A Conversation Book 1

English in Everyday Life
Third Edition

P9-CFY-701

Tina Kasloff Carver
Sandra Douglas Fotinos

Prentice Hall Regents
Englewood Cliffs, New Jersey 07632

Editorial Director: Arley Gray
Acquisitions editor: Nancy Baxer
Electonic technology production coordinator: Molly Pike Riccardi
Production supervision and desktop composition: Noël Vreeland Carter
Creative Director: Paula Ann Maylahn
Interior design: Noël Vreeland Carter
Cover design: Laura Ierardi
Electronic art: Wanda España
Pre-press/manufacturing buyer/Scheduler: Ray Keating

Art by Andrew Lang

© 1994 by Prentice Hall Regents
Prentice-Hall Inc.
A Paramount Communications Company
Englewood Cliffs, New Jersey 07632

Printed in the United States of America
10 9 8 7 6 5 4 3 2 1

0-13-053174-X

Prentice-Hall International (UK) Limited, London
Prentice-Hall of Australia Pty. Limited, Sydney
Prentice-Hall of Canada Inc. Toronto
Prentice-Hall Hispanoamericana, S.A., Mexico
Prentice-Hall of India Private Limited, New Delhi
Prentice-Hall of Japan, Inc. Tokyo
Simon & Schuster Asia Pte. Ltd., Singapore
Editora Prentice-Hall do Brasil, Ltda., Rio de Janeiro

CONTENTS

UNIT 1: WELCOME TO CLASS! 1

LESSON	COMPETENCY OBJECTIVES	PAGE
Welcome to Class!	• identify self and others • request and give information	2
Countries	• locate geographical areas	4
Numbers	• learn cardinal numbers • count	6
Journal	• express basic personal information and numbers in written form	7
Clothing and Colors	• identify articles of clothing and colors	8
Family	• identify immediate and extended family relationships	10
Review		12

UNIT 2: EVERYDAY LIFE 13

UNIT 3: THE CALENDAR <u>25</u>

UNIT 4: FOOD

41

UNIT 5: HOMES 61

UNIT 6: SHOPPING

UNIT 7: COMMUNITY

UNIT 8: WORK 127

UNIT 9: HEALTH 149

UNIT 10: LEISURE

FOREWORD

The third edition of **A CONVERSATION BOOK I** comes twenty years after the writing of the first. During these years, the field of ESL has changed greatly, but what students need to improve their skills in speaking English has remained the same. Students now, as then, need thought-provoking materials that will be of use to them in their daily lives. Students learn conversation skills best when the learning integrates their own experiences and interests.

We have incorporated the results of our experiences over the past twenty years in this revision. Although the physical appearance is different—the color, the art, the page composition—the philosophy remains the same. We have endeavored to bring to both student and teacher a plethora of topics and experiential material for study and practice. The materials are all student-centered. Although we have updated the methodology, changed much of the format and organization and added color as a pedagogical device, the basis for the text remains the same. We have developed a high frequency lexis within the context of everyday topics for low level students. As in earlier editions, the organization of the text provides for picking and choosing; the book is not spiraled in difficulty. We are providing a wide variety of springboards for teachers to design their curriculum according to the specific needs of their class. No two classes have the same needs—we have provided for that with a wide diversity of flexible and adaptable materials.

This third edition offers a special new feature—a modified picture dictionary base updated from the most successful pages of the previous editions. It also offers more directed activities and more specific instructions. We have carefully heeded the suggestions of our reviewers as well as the advice of teachers and students over the years.

We have also compiled a page-by-page **Teacher's Edition**, complete with ***Warm-up Activities***, *In the Text* suggestions and *Expansion Activities*. The **Teacher's Edition** also contains **Tests** for each Chapter. **Color Transparencies** for each Vocabulary page are available in a boxed set.

We hope you will enjoy using **A CONVERSATION BOOK I**, Third Edition, and that it will make your conversation class a meaningful, enjoyable and memorable learning experience for students and teacher alike.

ACKNOWLEDGMENTS

No book is ever written in isolation. We could never begin to cite all the teachers we have spoken with, the programs we have been able to observe and the authors who have influenced the writing of this book. They all have been part of our education and developing expertise as authors. We are indebted to them all, as well as to those teachers and students who have used the last two editions of the **CONVERSATION BOOK**.

The process of getting a book from first concept to press and out to the classroom involves many people. We were fortunate to have had dedicated, competent support during this time. Our sincere appreciation goes to Nancy Baxer, our editor. Noël Vreeland Carter, our designer and production editor, combined her remarkable skills in designing and editing with a great sensitivity to ESL and to the visual presentation, which has resulted in a masterfully produced book that is eminently student-friendly and usable. Andrew Lange, our artist, embarked on this venture with an open mind and a wonderful spirit, and has combined his creative artwork with understanding and humor. The result is a whole new artistic pedagogy—a major focus of change in the third edition.

Also, thanks to Barbara Barysh, Andy Martin, and Gil Muller, as well as H.T. Jennings, Karen Chiang and Norman Harris for their professional contributions and personal support.

A word of thanks to our reviewers for their assistance in pointing the way to us and for their constructive, helpful and supportive comments. Thanks to Ann Creighton, Edwina Hoffman, Laurie Ogilvie Lewis, Toni Hadi, Roni Lebauer, Barbara Wiggin, Greg Cossu, Kay Ferrell, and Kedre Murray.

Our own personal experiences as ESL teachers as well as foreign language learners underlie every page of **A CONVERSATION BOOK 1**. As learners, living and working in other countries, we were being reminded daily that learning a new culture and a new language is very hard work! To the many people who have afforded us friendship when we were far from home, helped us deal with the complexity of everyday life in a new place, and patiently shared perceptions and languages with us, thank you. Without those experiences and without those people to guide us along, **A CONVERSATION BOOK 1** would never have been written.

A Personal Word from Tina Carver

It is rare that an editor is afforded the opportunity to thank authors, but this time, the role reversal is appropriate. I have the good fortune to be associated with several people who professionally not only exhibit the highest level of excellence to which I aspire, but who, through the years, have also become very good friends. I will always value that friendship more than anything else. So, to Betty Azar, Bill Bliss, Doug Brown, Robert Lado and Steve Molinsky, thank you—so much of the improvement in this revision is the result of the many years of our professional conversations and work together.

A special note of appreciation goes to Sandra Fotinos, my master teacher of so many years ago, whose expert teaching and instincts towards students' needs have set an example to me throughout my career. Through all these years and experiences, both personal and professional, we have remained friends and colleagues.

I would like to express my appreciation to my three children, Jeffrey, Brian and Daniel. They were all barely pre-schoolers when the first edition was published. Now college students, they watched over my shoulder as the third edition came to fruition. Their daily help and understanding—from reading the manuscript and offering suggestions to doing the cooking, laundry, shopping, and walking the dogs—made my work easier and indeed, possible. My mother and father, Ruth and George Kasloff, influenced my early decision-making. My mother has continued to guide and to support me in all my endeavors. Finally, I would like to express my appreciation to Gene Podhurst for his cheerful and helpful contributions. He has read every page of the student text and the **Teacher's Edition** over and over—and over—again. His excellent suggestions and insightful comments on the pedagogy and the execution of the ideas have added greatly to the new level of interest and the improvements made in this third edition.

A Personal Word from Sandra Fotinos

As an ESL teacher by profession, I would like to thank my colleagues at Northern Essex Community College, Cochise College and Harvard University for the many good years of stories and teaching techniques that we have shared, and for the constant, gentle reminder that what works once does not necessarily work again in another class or for another teacher.

For whatever I have really learned of living across cultures and languages through the delights and the hard times of everyday life, I want to say thank you to my Fotinos family-by-marriage, and especially to my mother-in-law, Kleopatria Fotinou, of Kallitsaina, Messinias, who has been for nearly thirty years, my Greek teacher and a loving, understanding friend.

Finally, thank you again to my children, Christina, Elizabeth and Paul, who, like Tina's children, grew up with the **CONVERSATION BOOKS**, and whose cross-cultural life experiences are imbedded in so many of the conversations of the books. And, for the kind of personal support without which writing a book in one's "spare time" is impossible, thank you, Gene Riggs, Faye Douglas, Byron Berry, Jane Thiefels, and Tina Carver, my friend, publisher, and co-author.

New York/Arizona
June, 1993

xvi

NOTES TO THE TEACHER

These notes are provided as springboards for your own creativity and initiative. Our intention in writing A CONVERSATION BOOK 1 was to provide a wide variety of vocabulary and student-centered learning activities for you to use within your own style and that of your beginning and low intermediate students.

Equally important is creating an atmosphere of shared learning in which students' differences are valued and their life experiences are appreciated. Learning a foreign language is perhaps the most threatening of all disciplines yet among the most rewarding. In the conversation class, students need to feel the class is a partnership— one between teacher and student as well as between student and student.

THE FIRST CLASS

The most important goal on the first day is to set a supportive, non-threatening learning environment. The room should be appealing; if possible, provide a way of relaxation for the students (who may be quite anxious) such as playing music when they arrive and/or offering coffee and tea and a snack. This will prove to be a worthwhile investment of time and thought.

- Provide name tags for all students (either just first names or both first and last). Wear one yourself.
- Spend time talking with students before even tackling the first page of the text. (Perhaps you don't even want to use the text during the first class; instead, have an informal, ice breaking session. Use the material of the text but without the text itself.)
- Use yourself as a model. Try to scout any students who may know a little more and use them as models too.
- Introduce yourself, speaking slowly. Ask, **What's your name?** If a student doesn't understand, use another student as a model, or ask *yourself* and answer it as a model. Write the questions on the board to help students who may recognize written words but not be able to understand what you are saying. As the semester proceeds, both you and your students will learn to understand each other's speech. In the meantime, provide written reinforcement to reduce anxiety.

Suggestion

- Bring a large, lightweight ball to class.
- Have students stand in a circle. Participate in the first round.
- Hold the ball. Say your name and throw the ball to a student (STUDENT 1) you are relatively sure will respond.
- Motion to Student 1 to repeat your name.
- Have Student 1 say his/her name and throw the ball to another student (STUDENT 2) who says Student 1's name. Then as Student 2 throws the ball, he/she says his/her own name.
- Explain *throw* and *catch* by <u>doing</u> the actions.

This will be a gentle beginning into the more intricate movements of Total Physical Response (TPR) activities.

- Repeat the game until all students have had a chance or two to give their own name.

• Do this activity as an entire class or in groups, depending on the size of the class.

There is a "mascot" throughout the book. Sometimes he is sitting on the vocabulary boxes, sometimes he (she?) is sitting on the vocabulary boxes, sometimes he is integrated into the drawings. You and the class may want to <u>name</u> the mascot during the first session. This could be an enjoyable **Name Game.** Ask the class to suggest names for him. List the names on the board. Then vote on the names and give him the name the students select.

VOCABULARY

Although the lessons in A CONVERSATION BOOK 1 are designed for use either sequentially or in random order, the words are only listed once—the first time they appear. Keep this in mind if you are not using the book from beginning to end. Every lesson has at least one vocabulary box. The list in the box is *not* exhaustive, but it does give the basic vocabulary for the lesson. Although words are not repeated in the subsequent boxes, the *items* are found repeatedly throughout the text in the illustrations. For example, the word **shirt** appears first in the lesson on **CLOTHING** on page 8 in UNIT 1. The word does not appear in the vocabulary box in the **MEN'S CLOTHING STORE** lesson, but a shirt appears in the illustration on page 90. This device can serve as a review.

Use the **Index** to find the words and their original page references. This index is truly an *index*, and not a word list. Take the opportunity to teach the students about how and when an index can be used in their studies.

We have suggested a number of ways to present the vocabulary in the **Teacher's Edition**. Ultimately, the best methods depend upon your own style of teaching and the students' style of learning. You may want to discuss the illustration first, using the text or the transparency. This allows students to utilize what they know already and lets you assess the class' level of vocabulary proficiency. It also gives an immediate context for the vocabulary. Alternatively, you can simply point to each illustration and ask for the words. This way students associate the illustration with the English word. Combine methods for variety. Any method loses its effectiveness if used over and over agin.

In every vocabulary box there are lines for students to write vocabulary they contribute to the class discussion. These can be words they know already or words they want to learn (through a dictionary, other students or through you as the teacher-resource). Make these student-generated words part of the lesson too.

Modeling the words for pronunciation is useful for students so they can *hear* how to *say* the word in English along with *seeing* the illustration and the *written* word. Although sometimes it is difficult for you to hear all the pronunciations, choral repetition will give all students an opportunity to verbalize the words they are learning. Be sure students understand all the words. Sometimes native language translation is appropriate; that is your judgment call!

Note Taking

Suggest that students buy a notebook. Have students divide the notebook into four sections: **Vocabulary, Journal, Community Information, Activities.** When new words are generated in the classroom from discussion or from activities, students should record the words and information in the **Vocabulary** section of their notebooks. Write new words on the board for students to record more easily. The **Community Information** section should be a place to note valuable information about the students' communities. The **Activities section** should be used for any activities the students do in class or at home. There are specific suggestions in the **Teacher's Edition** as to how and when to use the notebook.

GRAMMAR

Grammar is not treated at all in the student book. In the **Teacher's Edition**, we have made reference to grammar chunks where necessary for clarification. You might want to teach and/or review a particular construction for an activity before or after the activity. The emphasis should be on conversation and communication, not grammatical accuracy.

CORRECTIONS

We are often asked how to handle corrections in the conversation class. Use your own best judgment. Too much correction inhibits students' ability to think coherently and works contrary to practicing coherent conversation skills. On the other hand, teachers should aim to strike a balance, teaching syntax as well as pronunciation at opportune times. Make a mental note of the errors students are making. It is usually not helpful to interrupt the flow of students conversations, but to correct errors at the appropriate time later in class, without referring to any specific students.

GROUPING

Pairing partners can be done in a variety of ways. The easiest way is to have students seated next to each other be partners. However, since an objective of the partner activities is for students to get to know one another, having a variety of partners is essential. Pairing students in different ways maintains students' attention, moves them around the room, and helps them to learn each other's names.

Suggestion:

- Count the students in the class; then divide them in half by left side/right side or front/back.
- Hand out little slips of paper to one half of the students.
- Ask them to write their whole names on the paper and fold the paper.
- Collect all the folded papers, then walk through the other half of the class. Have each student pick one folded paper.
- When all the papers are handed out, instruct the students with the papers to find their partners and sit down together.
- Depending on the class (and your own teaching style), you may prefer an open free-for-all with everyone walking around at once, calling out names, or a more structured pairing in which one student at a time reads the name on his or her paper, the student named raises his or her hand, and the two then sit together.

This method of pairing can be used again and again, dividing the class in different ways to assure that students have many different partners and get to know everyone in the class by name.

Partners should always ask each other for their names; there is a place in each **Partner Activity** for students to write their **Partner's Name**.

For some activities, larger groups of students are preferable. Again, grouping students can be done in a variety of ways.

Suggestion:

- Have students count off numbers, (1-4, 1-5, 1-6, etc.), then join the group that has their number.

- To practice vocabulary, you may replace numbers with items from the current vocabulary list—colors, fruits, vegetables, flowers, seasons, etc.
- List the group names on the board (for example, with colors, Red, Black, Yellow, Green, etc.), then assign each student a color and have students form groups, according to their assigned color.

After students get to know each other, informal methods of pairing or grouping usually work best. Sometimes you can let students choose a partner or set up their own groups. For other activities, depending on the subject matter, you may want to deliberately mix gender, ages, language groups, occupations, or opinions. Try to avoid cliques sitting together. Remind students that the only way to develop conversational fluency in English is to practice *in* English.

PARTNER ACTIVITIES

Partner activities give students non-threatening, one-on-one opportunities to interact on a personal level. They are the only activities in which every student in the class has to do 50% of the talking and has to listen on a one-on-one basis. We have included five types of partner activities: **Games, Interviews, Journals,** and **Role Plays.**

Games

There are two types of partner games: **Memory** games (**What do you remember?/ Same or different?/ Vocabulary Challenges**) and **Mime** games. Do a dry run with the class so that students understand what to do.

What do you remember? and Same or different?

- Divide the class into pairs.
- Discuss with the students how to remember the details of the illustration as they are looking at it. (How many people, colors, what season, what activities, etc.)
- Then have them close their texts and turn to the **Activities** section of their notebooks.
- Have the pairs work together, noting the differences in the illustrations. Have them number each difference so that it will be easy to count how many they have listed.
- When students have finished, have different pairs dictate to you the things they remember as you write them on the board.
- Open the texts or show the transparency. Look at the illustration together.
- Draw a line under the last item you have written and have students dictate additional items as you write them on the board.
- Point out new vocabulary for students to add to the **Vocabulary** section.

Mimes:

Sometimes students are asked to act out words or actions with a partner. Demonstrate the activity for the students first so they understand what to do. As the class is doing the activity, circulate; help students where needed.

Vocabulary Challenges

- Divide the class into pairs.
- Books must be closed. "Challenge" the pairs of students to make a list of as many vocabulary words and phrases as they remember from the lesson. Have them number

the words as they write. Give them a time limit for completing the list.

- When the time is up, ask how many words and phrases each pair had.
- Have a pair read their entire list. Copy it on the board. Star the words that are *not* from the lesson. Have the class check off the words they have on their lists.
- Have another pair read *only* the words they have that aren't on the board. List the new words on the board.
- Have the class check off the words they have that are on the board.
- Have another pair read new words from their list. List the new words on the board. Have the class check off any new words.
- Ask which other pair has new words. Add the words to the list.
- Ask which pair had the most new words. They "win" the challenge!

Interviews

It is important, especially during the first days of class, for the students to understand how to conduct these interviews. The teacher's role is to model pronunciation, facilitate understanding of vocabulary and questions and provide possible answers. For modeling, use a student who will catch on quickly; be careful not to use the same student all the time. Or, if it is more appropriate, model both roles yourself. Write the question and answer on the board so that students can *see* the questions and answers as well as *hear* them.

- Practice the interview questions with the students. Be sure they understand the questions and the vocabulary. Supply any additional words needed.
- Divide the class into pairs.
- Have students interview their partners. Circulate; help as needed.
- After partners conduct their interviews, have several pairs present their interviews for the class. Either have them present all questions or have different pairs of partners present one question each. Alternatively, have them share what they have learned about each other with another pair of students.
- Write new vocabulary generated from the interviews on the board. Have students copy the new words in their notebooks.
- Use the students' responses to the interviews for further discussions which may be of interest to the class.

Journals

The journal entries give students a chance to use the vocabulary and phrases they have learned in a writing reinforcement activity. Journals should be done as an interactive activity.

- Discuss the topic with the students before they write anything.
- Model and practice questions provided at the top of the page. Add your own questions if appropriate.
- Divide the class into pairs.
- Have partners ask each other the questions. Circulate; help as needed.
- Have students do their individual journal writing in class or at home.
- Have students proofread their journals.
- Partners should read their journals to each other and be encouraged to ask questions and make comments.
- If there is time, have several students read their journals to the class.

- Alternatively, read several journals to the class and have students guess who wrote them.
- Have one or two students put their journal entries on the board. Write the skeleton paragraph as it appears in the text. Either you or the student can fill in the blanks. Have students read what they wrote on the board, or you can read it as a model. Discuss new vocabulary and new ideas.
- Take advantage of any additional topics or information that may emerge to continue conversations and exchanges of information.
- Students can keep more journal pages in the **Journal** section of their notebooks. Provide guidance for the topics and do light corrections. The object of journal pages is for students to have practice writing fluently in English and expressing their thoughts and emotions. Too much correction will inhibit this goal.

Role Plays

Before students do role playing for the first time, do a sample role play using yourself and another student. This will provide a model for students when they are working independently.

- Divide the class into pairs.
- List the vocabulary needed on the board. Leave the vocabulary on the board as a reference for students when they are working with their partners.
- Students should write the conversation and practice reading their "scripts" with the "read and look up" technique. (*Scan the line; remember it as well as they can; look at the other person and SAY the line, don't read it—even beginners can perfect this technique. It helps with the appropriate eye contact and body language required in English.*)
- Have several pairs demonstrate their role plays—with simple props, if appropriate.
- It is always better to have the pair in the front of the room or in the middle of the circle rather than at their desks. Encourage this, although students may feel uncomfortable at first.
- For classes with shy students, an alternative to a traditional role play is a puppet show. Make hand puppets from small paper bags. Cover a table with a sheet for a stage. This activity can be simple or elaborate.

GROUP ACTIVITIES

Group activities give students a feeling of belonging and a feeling of being a part of the group's success. These activities allow students to get to know one another and to cooperate within the framework of different tasks. Many of the activities are cooperative; they require each member of the group to contribute something. While the groups are working, you can move from group to group as a facilitator to be sure students understand their task. After the groups do their activity, there should be a reporting back to the class as a whole so that there can be summation and conclusions can be drawn. We have included seven types of group activities: **Conversation Squares, Discussions, Gossip Games, Problem Posing/Solving, Surveys, Vocabulary Challenges** and **What's the Story?**

Conversation Squares

- Have the students help you create the question they will need to ask for each square.
- Write the questions on the board.

- Construct boxes on the board similar to the ones in the text.
- Choose two students. Use yourself as Number 1.
- Put the three names on the top of the boxes as indicated in the text.
- Ask and answer the questions for your box; write in your responses.
- Ask your partners the questions. Write in their responses.
- Then ask the class the questions for more practice.
- Have groups of three do the activity.
- When all students have finished, ask different groups single questions from the conversation squares. Put new vocabulary on the board for students to write in the **Vocabulary** section of their notebooks.

Discussions

These activities consist of guided questions. Each group should appoint a *leader* to ask the questions and a *recorder* to record the answers. That way, when called upon to recite, the answers are written down and students can feel confident in their replies. Real learning in these activities goes on within the group's dynamic. Reporting back is a way to summarize. Students shouldn't feel intimidated by the reporting back part of the activity. Writing answers usually eliminates this anxiety.

During the reporting back stage, note new vocabulary; write it on the board and have students write the new words **Vocabulary** section of their notebooks.

Gossip!

This is a variation of the "Gossip" or "Telephone" game. It has two objectives: to practice new vocabulary in context without visual cues and to demonstrate how information is lost in the process of retelling. A "**Secret** " for each game is included in the **Appendix**.

- Divide the class into large groups, or do this activity with the whole class, if your class is small.
- Use large groups for this activity—or the whole class, if your class is small.
- Use the illustration on the text's cover to explain the game. Start on the top left with the mascot. End on the bottom right with the mascot.
- Have the leader from each group read the **Secret** silently several times. All other should students have their books closed.
- Have the leaders close their books and quietly whisper the **Secret** to the student next to them. Those students quietly whisper it to the next, and so on. Be sure to explain the words "whisper" and "secret."
- When all students have heard the secret, have the last student of each group report the information to the class, either orally or in written form on the board.
- Have everyone read the **Secret** together to see what information was lost and changed.

Problem Posing/Problem Solving
- Divide the class into small groups.
- Do a practice problem posing/solving example with the class as a whole.
- Have each group choose a *recorder* and a *leader*. Each student should participate in some way.
- Before students begin, be sure that they understand the goal of the activity and that they have adequate vocabulary and grammar to do the work.
- Have students think about what is happening in the illustration and formulate a

question about it (pose the problem). Remind the leader to ask the questions.

- Then have them think through (analyze) the problem and as a group, decide what to do (solve the problem). This will take thought, negotiation, resolution and agreement.
- To summarize, have each group report back to the class.
- Draw class conclusions, even if there is diversity of opinion and resolution.

Surveys

This activity gives students the opportunity to give their own opinions and preferences, express their own, and check their accuracy in listening and recording answers.

- Model the questions; have students repeat; check pronunciation.
- Be sure students understand all the vocabulary and the objective of the activity before the activity starts.
- Have students check off their own answers in the appropriate column.
- Divide the class into groups of seven to ten. If your class is small, do the activity with the whole class
- Encourage the students to get up an walk around their group asking questions. Remind them that each student should ask everyone in the group all the questions and check the appropriate column for every answer.
- Set a time limit. Tell students to sit down when they finish and count their results. Remind them to include their own answers in the count.
- Have students report their results to their group. If other members of the group have different numbers, have them figure out who is right.
- While groups are working, copy the chart on the board.
- When groups are sure of their numbers, have them report their results. Fill in the columns on the board and have students draw conclusions about the class.
- Point out new words and have students write them in the **Vocabulary** section of their notebooks.

Vocabulary Challenge

This activity is similar to the **Vocabulary Challenges** as described in the **Memory Games** section of **PARTNERS ACTIVITIES**.

What's the Story?

This activity's goal is to have students look at an illustration (which tells a story), use their imaginations and their store of vocabulary to create their own story. These activities are cooperative learning activities. Each student should contribute one, two or three lines. The story should be complete and make sense.

- Divide the class into groups.
- Have each group select a *recorder* to write everyone's lines.
- Encourage students to help each other. Be sure that even the shy students participate by contributing their lines.
- After the stories are written, all groups should listen to their recorder read the story. They should all make changes and corrections and "edit" the story before the rest of the class hears it. Have another student (not the recorder) read the story, or have each student read or recite his/her lines.
- Have the class decide which was the best, the most exciting, the saddest, the funniest, etc.

CLASS ACTIVITIES

Class activities provide opportunities for lots of input; this is the advantage of a large class. Many opinions and many answers make the class more interesting and exciting. However, if your class functions better in smaller groups, these activities can work as Group Activities also. We have included seven types of class activities: **Community Activities, Cross-Cultural Exchanges, Discussions, Find Someone Who, Strip Stories, Total Physical Response Activities (TPR),** and **Vocabulary Challenges.**

Community Activities

These activities give the class the opportunity to go out into the community and explore, as well as to explore community resources (i.e., the telephone book) in the classroom itself. Students can be sent out individually, in groups or with partners to gather information requested.

- Review the task before students are asked to do the work independently. Be sure students know the vocabulary and are clear about what they are to do.
- To help prepare students, role play expected outcomes. This may avoid pitfalls and panic!
- If possible, accompany the class the first time out. This will give them confidence.
- After the students do the assignment, review it in class.
- Discuss not only the task but what happened—what surprises they had, what reactions they had, how they felt, etc.
- Have student keep important community information in the **Community** section of their notebooks.

Cross-cultural Exchanges

This activity gives the class the opportunity to talk about cultural differences in general as well as about US/Canadian cultures. Students should be encouraged to voice their opinions and confusions about cultures they associate with the English language. Opportunities and interest in this activity will vary with your classes. Wherever possible, compare three or more cultures rather than just two to avoid potential "either/or" interpretations of differences. Encourage inter-cultural openness and awareness without judgment.

Discussion

Ask the guided questions and choose different students to answer each question. This provides a model for the students. As an alternative approach, you can ask the first question and choose a student to answer. Then have that student ask the second question and choose a student to answer. Continue the pattern. Correct only large errors that impede understanding.

To help structure discussions and teach note taking skills, write a brief heading for each question on the board. Encourage students to do the same in the **Activities** section of their notebooks. List information you gather from the discussions under each heading.Then review your notes and ask the students to review theirs. Draw conclusions together from the notes at the end of the discussion.

Find Someone Who

This activity is similar to the **Survey** activity except in this activity, students are searching for "Yes" answers.

- Review the vocabulary and create the Yes/No questions with the class before they start the activity. Write the questions on the board.
- You might want to give students the grammar constructions in chunks.
- Have the class ask the questions by circulating around the class. If the class is very large, break the class into groups of 10–15 and have students do the activity within their group.
- When students have completed their work, have them sit in their seats.
- Review the questions and answers. There should be interesting springboards of conversation that come from the individual answers.

Strip Stories

This visual presentation of little stories gives students the opportunity to discuss the action in the frames and then to write their own captions.

- Have students look at the illustrations and discuss them together. Write vocabulary words on the board.
- Ask for suggestions for captions and/or bubbles.
- Write different suggestions on the board. Have students decide which one is best and why.
- Have students write captions in their texts.
- Alternatively, have students create captions individually, in groups or with partners.

Total Physical Response (TPR) activities

For the first Total Physical Response (TPR) activity, we have illustrated the steps. (See page 5 of the Student Text.) After that, the *instructions only* are in the text.

- Prepare students by giving out slips of paper that they will write something on—an instruction, a favorite month, a favorite food, etc.
- Always model the action before asking students to do it. The object of this activity is for students to associate the action with the words for it. Use exaggerated movements.
- After you do the action, have the class do the action.
- To review, have a student read the actions and have the class follow the instruction. Alternatively, have one half of the class read and the other half respond
- As a written review, dictate the actions and have students write the dictation in the **Activities** section of their notebooks.

Vocabulary Challenges

This activity is similar to the **Vocabulary Challenges** as described in the **Memory Games** section of PARTNERS ACTIVITIES.

INDIVIDUAL ACTIVITIES

These activities are designed for students to have the opportunity to share their individual perceptions, knowledge and experiences with the whole class. There are three types of individual activities: **Draw, Speeches** and **Tell the Class.**

Draw

Students don't have to be artists—nor do you—to do this. A rendition of what is called for is good enough for students to be able to talk about the drawings.

- Give students enough time to complete their drawing.
- Circulate; help where needed, but also scout students who will be able to share a useful drawing—either on the board, a transparency or xerox copies.
- Use your own artwork—the "worse" it is, sometimes, the better. Students are less reluctant to share theirs if yours *isn't* "good!"
- Have students talk about what they drew. Be sure to note new vocabulary words.

Speeches

Students get practice in simple speech writing and recitation with these activities. Give students ample time to prepare. Make the activity VERY structured and help correct as much as you can. Visual aids can help relieve anxiety. Allow students to have note cards, but not to read their speech. Sometimes it is helpful for students to practice with a partner or a small group before addressing the class. There are **Speech** and **Audience Evaluation forms** in the **Appendix**.

Tell the Class

These activities give students the opportunity to be in front of the class and speak without much preparation. With some notes, a little confidence, and a supportive environment, their anxiety levels will be lowered.

TEACHER'S EDITION

The page-for-page **Teacher's Edition** provides objectives and step-by-step suggestions for all **In the Text** activities. In addition, it provides **Warm-Up** and **Expansion** activities for each lesson. **Conversation** and **Vocabulary tests** for each unit are included in the back of the **Teacher's Edition**.

Transparencies

A boxed set of **Color Transparencies** is available. These transparencies include **ALL** the illustrations from the picture dictionary pages as well as other illustrations which lend themselves to class discussions. The transparencies can facilitate the introduction of the vocabulary lesson by allowing students to close their books and look up rather than being engrossed in words and page turning. The transparencies focus students' attention and enable teachers to point out details more easily. The transparencies can also be used for class activities and for vocabulary review.

UNIT 1

Welcome to Class

1

WELCOME TO CLASS!

Draw

Draw a picture of yourself.

1. woman
2. man
3. girl
4. boy

5. single
6. married
7. divorced
8. widowed

9. hair
10. long
11. short
12. curly
13. wavy
14. straight

15. eyes
16. brown
17. blue
18. gray
19. green

20. glasses
21. earrings
22. moustache
23. beard

_____
_____
_____
_____
_____
_____

Write

My name is _____.

1. I am a _____.

2. I am _____.

3. My hair is _____.

4. My eyes are _____.

5. I have _____.

2

Tell the Class *

Write your first name and your last name on the board. • *Tell the class your name.* • *Show your picture to the class.* • *Describe your picture.*

Partner Activity

Partner's name _____

Introduce yourself to your partner. • *Practice all these ways.*

A: My name is _____. What's your name? (*or*)
Hello. I'm _____. What's your name? (*or*)
Hi. I'm _____. What is your name?

B: Nice to meet you. My name is _____. (*or*)
I'm _____. I'm pleased to meet you.

Introduce your partner to the class.

I'd like you to meet _____. (*or*)
This is _____.

Group Activity

Work in groups of three or four. • *Write a name tag for yourself.* • *Pronounce the names of each student in your group.* • *Introduce yourself to the others in the group.*

* *See Appendix page 197 for Names/Nicknames.*

3

COUNTRIES

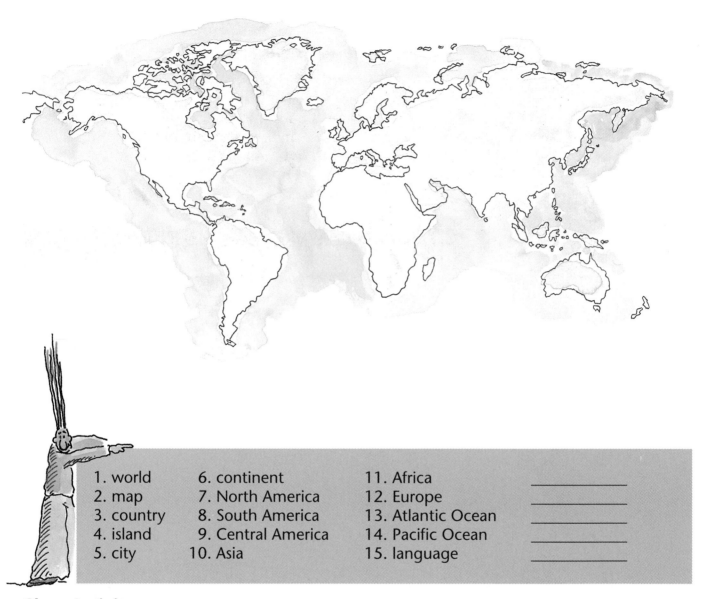

1. world	6. continent	11. Africa	_____
2. map	7. North America	12. Europe	_____
3. country	8. South America	13. Atlantic Ocean	_____
4. island	9. Central America	14. Pacific Ocean	_____
5. city	10. Asia	15. language	_____

Class Activity

Find your country on the map. • Circle the places on your map where all your classmates are from. • Draw a big star where you are now.

Partner Interview*

Partner's Name _____

Practice these questions with your teacher. • Then ask your partner.

1. What is your name?
2. What country are you from?
3. What city are you from?
4. What continent are you from?
5. Where do you live now?
6. What languages do you speak?

Tell the Class

Tell the class about your partner.

✳ See Appendix page 198 for Nations/Nationalities.

4

Class Game*: *"Where do you want to visit?"*

1. Think.

4. Make a pile.

2. Write.

5. Open one. Read it to the class.

3. Fold.

6. Guess who wrote it.

Tell the Class

Tell the class about the place you want to visit.

* *See Appendix pages 192–196 for Maps.*

NUMBERS

0 zero	9 nine	18 eighteen	27 twenty-seven
1 one	10 ten	19 nineteen	28 twenty-eight
2 two	11 eleven	20 twenty	29 twenty-nine
3 three	12 twelve	21 twenty-one	30 thirty
4 four	13 thirteen	22 twenty-two	40 forty
5 five	14 fourteen	23 twenty-three	50 fifty
6 six	15 fifteen	24 twenty-four	60 sixty
7 seven	16 sixteen	25 twenty-five	70 seventy
8 eight	17 seventeen	26 twenty-six	80 eighty

90 ninety
100 one hundred
_____
_____

Class Activity

Count the men and women in your class. • *Write the correct number and word for each question.* • *Report your answers to the class.*

	MEN	WOMEN
1. How many are there?	_____	_____
2. How many have  ?	_____	_____
3. How many are ?	_____	_____
4. How many have blue ?	_____	_____
5. How many have ?	_____	_____
6. How many have ?	_____	_____
7. How many have a  ?	_____	_____
TOTALS	_____	_____

Group Activity

Work in groups of four. • *Write the names of all the students in your group.* • *Write what you remember about each student.* • *Compare notes with your group.* • *Read your group list to the class.*

6

JOURNAL

Partner Interview

Partner's Name _____

Practice these questions with your teacher. •
Then ask your partner.

1. What is today's date?
2. How many students are in our class?
3. What is your name?
4. What color is your hair?
5. What color are your eyes?
6. Are you married or single?
7. Where are you from?
8. What language do you speak?

Write

Write about your partner.

Journal

_____
(1)

I am in my English class. There are _____ students
(2)

in my class today. My partner's name is._____
(3)

She/He has_____ hair and _____ eyes.
(4)   (5)

My partner is _____. She/He is from _____ and
(6)   (7)

speaks _____.
(8)

Tell the Class

Read your journal to the class • *Tell the class about your partner.*

CLOTHING AND COLORS

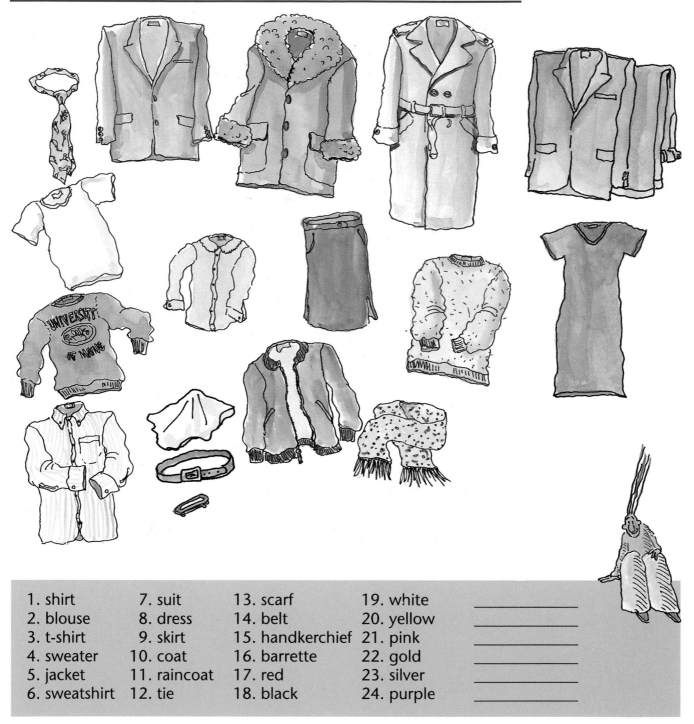

1. shirt	7. suit	13. scarf	19. white
2. blouse	8. dress	14. belt	20. yellow
3. t-shirt	9. skirt	15. handkerchief	21. pink
4. sweater	10. coat	16. barrette	22. gold
5. jacket	11. raincoat	17. red	23. silver
6. sweatshirt	12. tie	18. black	24. purple

Partner Game: "What do you remember?"   Partner's name _____

Look at your partner's clothing. • Sit back to back. • Make a list of what your partner is wearing. • Read your list to your partner. • Don't look at your partner. • Correct your list with your partner.

Class Activity

List the different colors the class is wearing on the board. • How many men are wearing each color? • How many women are wearing each color? • What is the class' favorite color?

8

PAIRS OF CLOTHING

1. shoes	8. socks	15. panties	_____
2. sandals	9. pants (slacks)	16. gloves	_____
3. sneakers	10. jeans	17. mittens	_____
4. boots	11. shorts	18. sunglasses	_____
5. slippers	12. pajamas	19. old	_____
6. stockings	13. jockey shorts	20. new	_____
7. panty hose	14. boxer shorts	21. pair	_____

Group Game: *"True or false?"*

Work in groups of four. • *Write three true statements about your clothes.* • *Write one false statement.* • *Read your statements to your group.* • *Who can guess the false statement?*

Group Game: *"What am I wearing?"*

Describe one student's clothing from outside your group. • *Who can guess that student's name?*

FAMILY

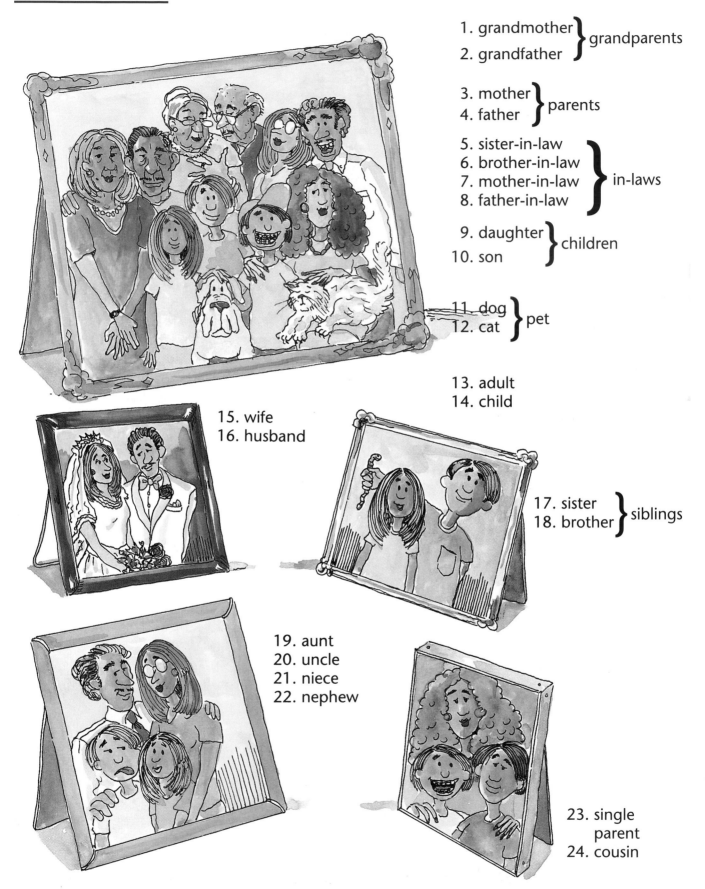

1. grandmother } grandparents
2. grandfather

3. mother } parents
4. father

5. sister-in-law
6. brother-in-law } in-laws
7. mother-in-law
8. father-in-law

9. daughter } children
10. son

11. dog } pet
12. cat

13. adult
14. child

15. wife
16. husband

17. sister } siblings
18. brother

19. aunt
20. uncle
21. niece
22. nephew

23. single parent
24. cousin

Tell the Class

Can you add more words to the list? • *Tell the class about a favorite person in your family.*

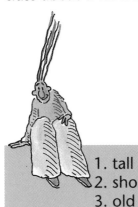

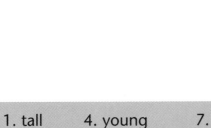

1. tall	4. young	7. medium	10. sympathetic	_____
2. short	5. thin	8. blonde	11. funny	_____
3. old	6. heavy	9. helpful	12. wise	_____

Partner Interview

Partner's name _____

Practice these questions with your teacher. • *Then ask your partner.*

1. Is your family big or small?
2. How many people are in your family?
3. How many brothers and sisters do you have?

4. Are they older or younger?
5. Do you have children?
6. Do you have a pet?

Draw

Work in groups of four or five. • *Draw a family portrait or a family tree.* • *Tell your group about your family.*

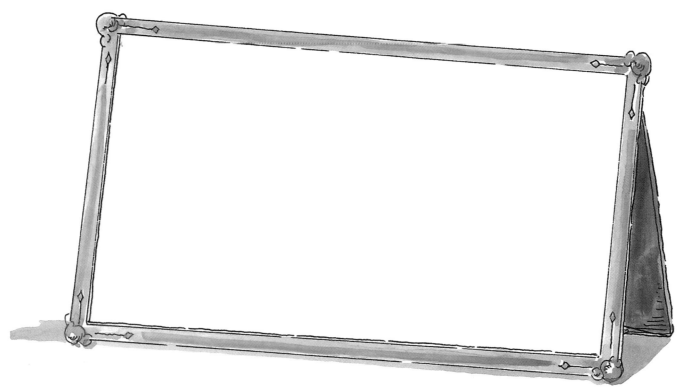

Tell the Class

Bring in photos of your family. • *Show your photos to the class.* • *Explain who everyone is.*

THE CLASSROOM

1. classroom	8. wall	15. pencil	_____
2. window	9. door	16. paper	_____
3. board	10. chair	17. book	_____
4. floor	11. map	18. clock	_____
5. ceiling	12. notebook	19. teacher	_____
6. table	13. eraser	20. student	_____
7. desk	14. pen	21. chalk	_____

Draw

Draw a picture of your classroom.• Include everything. • Work fast! • Compare pictures with the class. • Who had the most complete picture ?

Group Game: *"What is it?"*

Work in groups of six.
Choose a leader.

      Leader: *Think about something in the classroom. Don't say it!*
       Class: *Ask the leader YES/NO questions.*
      Leader: *Answer "yes" or "no".*
       Class: *Try to guess what it is. Whoever guesses is the new leader.*

15

TAKING A BREAK

1. waving	7. writing	13. arguing	19. coming in _____
2. shaking hands	8. drawing	14. frowning	20. walking _____
3. talking	9. erasing	15. worrying	21. sitting _____
4 looking	10. laughing	16. crying	22. standing _____
5. listening	11. speaking	17. thinking	23. sleeping _____
6. reading	12. smiling	18. going out	24. yawning _____

Class Game: *"What am I doing?"*

Think. • *Write an activity.* • *Fold your paper.* • *Make a pile of papers.* • *Open one.* • *Follow the instruction.* • *Ask "What am I doing?"* • *Have the class guess the activity.*

Partner Game: *"How are you today?"*   Partner's Name. _____

Decide how these students are today. • *Give them names.* • *Write in the bubbles.* • *Draw and fill in your own.*

1. happy	4. hungry	7. hot _____
2. tired	5. thirsty	8. cold _____
3. angry	6. sick	9. nervous _____

Group Vocabulary Challenge

Work in groups of four. • *What do you do on a break?* • *Make a list with your group.* • *Read your group's list to the class.* • *With the class, make a list of the new words on the board.* • *Copy the new words into your notebook.*

17

EVERYDAY LIFE

A Mother's Day

A Worker's Day

1. sweeps the floor	6. feeds the baby	11. does laundry
2. takes a break	7. goes shopping	12. gets a paycheck
3. goes to work	8. makes dinner	13. reads to the children
4. punches in	9. goes to school	14. works
5. washes the dishes	10. does homework	

_____
_____
_____
_____
_____

Class Discussion

Decide the correct time for each activity. • Fill in the clocks. • Compare the everyday life of the mother and the worker.

Draw

Draw and write about your day.

1. _____	2. _____	3. _____	4. _____

5. _____	6. _____	7. _____	8. _____

Partner Activity

Partner's Name _____

Compare your day with your partner's day. • *What is the same?* • *What is different?*

SAME	DIFFERENT
1. _____	_____
2. _____	_____
3. _____	_____

Find Someone Who

Review the vocabulary with your teacher. • *Fill in the name of someone who . . .*

1. _____ washes the dishes every evening.
2. _____ makes dinner at home.
3. _____ punches in at work.
4. _____ does the laundry.

MORNING ROUTINE

1. brush his teeth
2. comb (his) hair
3. drink coffee
4. get dressed
5. get out of bed
6. leave for work
7. make the bed
8. read the newspaper
9. say goodbye
10. shave
11. take a shower
12. watch the news

What's The Story?

Work in groups of three. • *Write a story about the man.* • *Everyone in the group should contribute three sentences.* • *Read your story to the class.*

Group Game: *"What do you do in the morning?"*

Work in groups of five. • *Pantomime one of these activities for your group.* • *No speaking!* • *Whoever guesses takes the next turn.*

Get out of bed.
Make the bed.
Take a shower.
Shave.
Comb your hair.
Brush your teeth.
Read the newspaper.
Watch TV.
Drink coffee.
Leave for school.

BIRTHDAYS

1. party	8. horn	15. napkin
2. celebrate	9. decorations	16. table
3. surprise	10. paper plate	17. make a wish
4. cake	11. cup	18. blow out the candles
5. candle	12. spoon	19. Happy Birthday!
6. party hat	13. knife	20. present
7. balloon	14. fork	21. punch

What's the Story?

Work in groups of four. • *Write a story about the birthday party.* • *Everyone in the group should contribute at least one sentence.* • *Read your story to the class.*

1. What kind of celebration is this?
2. Whose birthday do you think it is?
3. How old is s/he?
4. What is on the table?
5. What do you think the presents are?

What's The Story?

Work in groups of three. • *Write a story about the man.* • *Everyone in the group should contribute three sentences.* • *Read your story to the class.*

Group Game: "What do you do in the morning?"

Work in groups of five. • *Pantomime one of these activities for your group.* • *No speaking!* • *Whoever guesses takes the next turn.*

Get out of bed.
Make the bed.
Take a shower.
Shave.
Comb your hair.
Brush your teeth.
Read the newspaper.
Watch TV.
Drink coffee.
Leave for school.

23

REVIEW

Group Vocabulary Challenge

Work in groups of five. • Make a list of all the vocabulary from your classroom. • Compare your list with another group. • Which group had more new words? • With the class, make a list of the new words on the board. • Copy the new words into your notebook.

Class Activity

List ten questions about your day. • Write them on the board.

Partner Activity   Partner's Name _____

Ask your partner the questions from the Class Activity. • Present your interview to the class.

Partner Game: *"What do you do every day"?*   Partner's Name_____

Take turns. • Pantomime what you do every day. • No speaking! • Let your partner guess. • List five of the activities. • Show your class what your partner does every day.

UNIT 3

The Calendar

DAYS OF THE WEEK

	SUNDAY	MONDAY	TUESDAY	WEDNESDAY	THURSDAY	FRIDAY	SATURDAY
MORNING							
AFTERNOON							
EVENING							

1. Sunday
2. Monday
3. Tuesday
4. Wednesday
5. Thursday
6. Friday
7. Saturday

8. today
9. yesterday
10. tomorrow
11. the day before yesterday
12. the day after tomorrow

13. calendar
14. week
15. week day
16. week-end
17. ago
18. last
19. next

_____
_____
_____
_____
_____
_____
_____

Write

What are you doing every day this week? • *Fill in the calendar.* • *Explain it to your partner.*

26

Partner Interview

Practice these questions with your teacher. • *Then ask your partner.*

1. What is today?
2. What day is tomorrow?
3. What day was yesterday? What did you do yesterday?
4. What day was the day before yesterday?
5. What are you going to do next week end?
6. What did you do last weekend?
7. Did you come to class last week?
8. Which is your favorite day? Why?
9. What are the days of the week.

Group Survey

Ask everyone in your group these questions. • *Check YES, NO or SOMETIMES.* • *Count the answers.* • *Report your group results to the class.* • *Write the class results on the board.*

Do you:	YES	NO	SOMETIMES
1. sleep late on Sundays?	_____	_____	_____
2. shop on Saturday afternoons?	_____	_____	_____
3. study late in the evening?	_____	_____	_____
4. go to the movies on Friday evenings?	_____	_____	_____
5. work on the week-ends?	_____	_____	_____

27

MONTHS AND DATES

JANUARY	FEBRUARY	MARCH	APRIL
MAY	JUNE	JULY	AUGUST
SEPTEMBER	OCTOBER	NOVEMBER	DECEMBER

first (1st)	eleventh (11th)	twenty-first (21st)	month
second(2nd)	twelfth (12th)	twenty-second (22nd)	year
third (3rd)	thirteenth(13th)	twenty-third (23rd)	leap year
fourth (4th)	fourteenth (14th)	twenty-fourth (24th)	century
fifth (5th)	fifteenth (15th)	twenty-fifth (25th)	
sixth (6th)	sixteenth (16th)	twenty-sixth (26th)	
seventh (7th)	seventeenth (17th)	twenty-seventh (27th)	
eighth (8th)	eighteenth (18th)	twenty-eighth (28th)	
ninth (9th)	nineteenth (19th)	twenty-ninth (29th)	
tenth (10th)	twentieth (20th)	thirtieth (30th)	
		thirty-first (31)	

Class Discussion

1. What is the date today?
2. What was last month?
3. What is next month?
4. What date does this course end?
5. What is the date of the next holiday?
6. When is the next leap year?
7. What century is this?

Group Activity

Work in groups of five or six. • *Decide on important dates.* • *Write them on your calendars.* • *Compare your dates with the class.*

Include:

1. your birthdays
2. other important dates
3. important holidays in your countries

Class Game: *"What is your favorite month?"*

Think. • *Write.* • *Fold.* • *Make a pile.* • *Open one.* • *Read it to the class.* • *Guess who wrote it.*

BIRTHDAYS

1. party
2. celebrate
3. surprise
4. cake
5. candle
6. party hat
7. balloon
8. horn
9. decorations
10. paper plate
11. cup
12. spoon
13. knife
14. fork
15. napkin
16. table
17. make a wish
18. blow out the candles
19. Happy Birthday!
20. present
21. punch

_____
_____
_____
_____
_____
_____
_____

What's the Story?

Work in groups of four. • *Write a story about the birthday party.* • *Everyone in the group should contribute at least one sentence.* • *Read your story to the class.*

1. What kind of celebration is this?
2. Whose birthday do you think it is?
3. How old is s/he?
4. What is on the table?
5. What do you think the presents are?

30

Partner Interview

Practice these questions with your teacher. • *Then ask your partner.*

1. What do you like to give as a birthday gift: to a friend? to a parent? to a co-worker? to a teacher? to a child?
2. When is your birthday? (or your name day?)
3. What kind of birthday cake is your favorite?
4. Describe how you like to celebrate your birthday (or your name day).

Write

Partner's name_____

When is your partner's birthday? • *Write a message to your partner on the card.* • *Sign the birthday card.* • *Give it to your partner.* • *Read your message to your partner.*

Cross-Cultural Exchange

Do people celebrate birthdays in your country? • *Do they celebrate name days?* • *Tell the class how they celebrate.* • *How do you say "Happy Birthday" in your native language?* • *Teach the class.*

HOLIDAYS

Date: _____

Date _____

Date: _____

Date: _____

1. New Year's Eve
2. champagne
3. streamers
4. Happy New Year!

5. Valentine's Day
6. chocolates
7. flowers
8. I love you!
9. Happy Valentine's Day!

10. Independence Day
11. flag
12. parade
13. fireworks
14. band

17. Halloween
18. jack-o'-lantern
19. pumpkin
20. ghost
21. witch
22. costume
23. Trick or Treat!
24. Happy Halloween!

Date: _____

Date: _____

25. Thanksgiving	31. Christmas
26. turkey	32. tree
27. apple pie	33. Christmas lights
28. Pilgrims	34. Santa Claus
29. settlers	35. Merry Christmas!
30. Native Americans	

Class Activity

Fill in the dates this year with your class. • What is your favorite holiday? • Tell the class.

Conversation Squares

Work in groups of three. • First write your own answers. • Then ask your partners the questions. • Write their answers. • Compare your group answers with other groups.

Favorite	You _____	Partner 1_____	Partner 2_____
holiday	_____	_____	_____
holiday food	_____	_____	_____
holiday activity	_____	_____	_____

Cross-Cultural Exchange

How do you say "Merry Christmas" and "Happy New Year" in your native language? • Make a list on the board. • Teach it to the class. • Do you know a holiday song from your country? • Sing it for the class.

Speech

Tell the class about your favorite holiday. • Include the date, special activities, holiday food and decorations.

SEASONS

1. apple trees	8. water	15. leaf	20. snow
2. cherry trees	9. sand	16. rake	21. snowsuit
3. nest	10. waves	17. harvest	22. snowman
4. bird	11. picnic basket	18. cider	23. snowball
5. egg	12. beach towel	19. farm stand	24. shovel
6. garden	13. volleyball		25. plow
7. beach			26. ice

34

Class Discussion

1. Where you live now, are the seasons the same as in the pictures?
2. What happens in each season?
3. What do you like to do in each season?
4. Which season is your favorite?
5. Are the seasons the same in your native city? What is different? What is the same?

What's the Story?

Work in groups of three. • Choose one season. • Write a story. • Everyone in the group should contribute at least two sentences • Read your story to the class.

1. What are the people wearing?
2. What are they doing?
3. Do they like what they are doing?

Partner Game: *"What do you remember?"*   Partner's name _____

Look at the picture with your partner. • Remember as much as you can. • Close your book. • Describe the picture with your partner. • List everything • Compare your notes with another pair of students. • Add to your list.

WEATHER

1. clear	7. cactus	13. bench	19. hail	25. hat
2. cloud	8. cowboy	14. puddle	20. hailstorm	26. muffler
3. grass	9. dust storm	15. rain	21. lightning	_____
4. hill	10. horse	16. splash	22. picnic	_____
5. shine	11. saddle	17. umbrella	23. thunder	_____
6. warm	12. wind	18. wet	24. earmuffs	_____

Class Discussion

What are the people doing in the pictures? • *What are they thinking?*

36

Partner Interview

Partner's name _____

Practice these questions with your teacher. • *Then ask your partner.*

What do you like to do:

1. on a rainy day?
2. on a sunny day?

3. on a cold day?
4. in the snow?

Find Someone Who

Review the vocabulary with your teacher. • *Fill in the name of someone who . . .*

1. _____ has never seen snow.
2. _____ has been in a dust storm.
3. _____ has been in a thunderstorm.
4. _____ likes rain.
5. _____ likes winter.
6. _____ likes to be outdoors in cold weather.
7. _____ likes to be outdoors in hot weather.
8. _____ has been in a hailstorm.

WEATHER REPORT

1. weather map	8. cloudy	15. east
2. meteorologist	9. showers	16. west
3. cool	10. thunderstorm	17. southeast
4. rainy	11. snowflakes	18. northeast
5. mild	12. temperature	19. southwest
6. dry	13. north	20. northwest
7. sunny	14. south	21. midwest

Group Discussion

Work in groups of five. • Look at the weather map. • Report on the weather in the following areas. • Compare your answers with the others in the class.

1. the northeast
2. the southeast
3. the southwest
4. the northwest
5. the midwest

Community Activities

Bring in a weather report from either a native language or an English newspaper. • Compare your report with others in the class.

Watch a weather report on tv. • Take notes:

1. What channel did you watch?
2. What time was the report on?
3. Who was the meteorologist?
4. What was the weather report for today?
5. Was it accurate?

SEASONAL CLOTHING

1. long underwear	6. bathing suit	11. halter
2. ski jacket	7. bikini	12. poncho
3. stocking cap	8. swim trunks	13. slicker
4. ski pants	9. cutoffs	14. rubbers
5. vest	10. tank top	

_____
_____
_____
_____
_____

Partner Interview

Partner's name _____

Practice these questions with your teacher. • Then ask your partner.

1. What do you wear in cold weather?
2. What do you wear when it rains?
3. What do you wear in hot weather?
4. What do you wear when you go to the beach?
5. What do you wear when you go on a picnic?

Speech

Tell the class about the weather in your hometown. • Use these questions as a guide:

1. Are there seasons in your hometown? What are they? When are they?
2. What is the weather like in each season?
3. What do people wear in each season?

REVIEW

Partner Interview

Partner's name _____

Ask your partner.

1. What is today's date?
2. What's the weather like today?
3. Is it hot? cold? warm? cool?
4. What season is it?
5. Do you like this weather?
6. What do you want to do today?

Write

Write in your journal.

Journal

_____
(1)

Today is a _____ day. It is
(2)

_____ during this season of _____.
(3)   (4)

I _____ the weather
(5)

today. It is a good day to _____.
(6)

Tell Your Partner

Read your journal entry to your partner. • *Listen to your partner's journal.*

UNIT 4

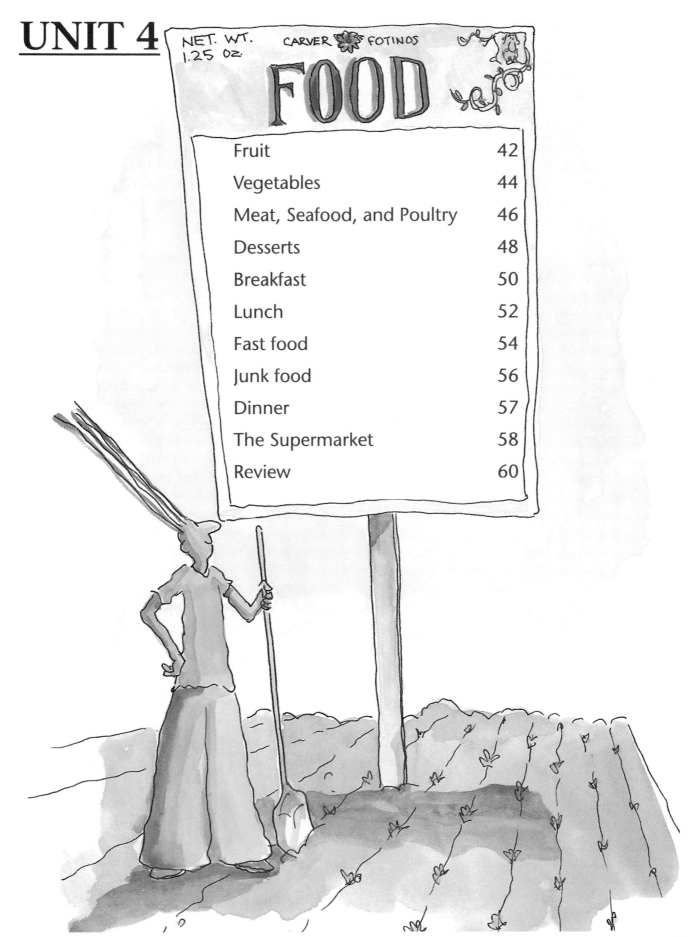

NET. WT.
1.25 oz.

CARVER ❀ FOTINOS

FOOD

FRUIT

1. apple	8. coconut	15. orange	22. strawberry	29. pound
2. apricot	9. grape	16. peach	23. watermelon	_____
3. banana	10. grapefruit	17. pear	24. seeds	_____
4. blackberry	11. kiwi	18. papaya	25. pit	_____
5. blueberry	12. lemon	19. pineapple	26. skin	_____
6. cantaloupe	13. lime	20. plum	27. box	_____
7. cherry	14. mango	21. raspberry	28. bunch	_____

Partner Interview

Practice these questions with your teacher. • *Then ask your partner.*

1. What is your favorite fruit?
2. What other fruits do you like?
3. What fruits grow in your country?
4. What fruits can you buy in your neighborhood?

Group Game: *"Preparing Fruit Salad"*

Work in groups of four. • *Plan to prepare a fruit salad for the next class.*

To Get Ready:

What fruit will each student bring?

_____   _____

_____   _____

Who will bring a bowl?   _____
Who will bring a knife?   _____
Who will bring a large spoon?   _____
Who will bring a fork?   _____

To Demonstrate:

• Prepare your fruit salad.

• Compare the fruit salads.

• Vote on the best one.

To Eat

• Enjoy the snack!

VEGETABLES

1. artichoke
2. bean
3. beet
4. broccoli
5. cabbage
6. carrot
7. celery
8. corn
9. cucumber
10. lettuce
11. mushroom
12. onion
13. peas
14. pepper
15. potato
16. tomato
17. head
18. ear

Partner Interview

Practice these questions with your teacher. • *Then ask your partner.*

1. What is your favorite vegetable?
2. What vegetables don't you like?
3. What vegetables grow in your country?
4. Which vegetables do you usually use for salad?
5. What do these vegetables usually cost at your market?
6. Which vegetables do you buy by the bunch? by the head? by the ear? by the pound?

Group Decision

Work in groups of five or six. • *Decide which vegetables to use for a salad.* • *Decide how to prepare each vegetable.* • *Tell the class about your salad.*

VEGETABLE	YES/NO	COOKED	RAW	PEELED	SLICED	SHREDDED
	_____	_____	_____	_____	_____	_____
	_____	_____	_____	_____	_____	_____
	_____	_____	_____	_____	_____	_____
	_____	_____	_____	_____	_____	_____
	_____	_____	_____	_____	_____	_____
	_____	_____	_____	_____	_____	_____
	_____	_____	_____	_____	_____	_____
	_____	_____	_____	_____	_____	_____
other	_____	_____	_____	_____	_____	_____
TOTALS	_____	_____	_____	_____	_____	_____

MEAT, SEAFOOD, AND POULTRY

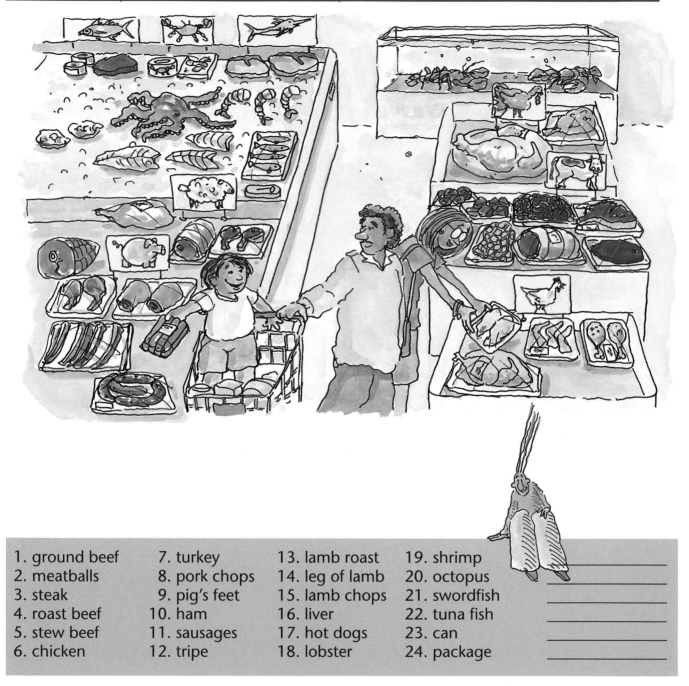

1. ground beef	7. turkey	13. lamb roast	19. shrimp
2. meatballs	8. pork chops	14. leg of lamb	20. octopus
3. steak	9. pig's feet	15. lamb chops	21. swordfish
4. roast beef	10. ham	16. liver	22. tuna fish
5. stew beef	11. sausages	17. hot dogs	23. can
6. chicken	12. tripe	18. lobster	24. package

Partner Interview

Partner's name _____

Practice these questions with your teacher. • *Then ask your partner.*

1. Do you eat meat? What is your favorite meat?
2. Do you eat poultry? What is your favorite?
3. Do you eat seafood? What is your favorite fish? What is your favorite shellfish?
4. Which meats, fish and poultry are most common in your country?
5. Are there any meats, fish or poultry that you never eat? Why?
6. Where do you buy meats? fish? poultry?
7. Is it a good idea to eat a lot of red meat? Why? Why not?

1. bake	4. fry	7. boil	10. seasoning
2. broil	5. simmer	8. barbeque	_____
3. roast	6. stir fry	9. casserole	_____

Find Someone Who

How do you like your food prepared? • *Review the vocabulary with your teacher.* • *Fill in the name of someone who . . .*

1. _____ likes baked fish with salt and pepper.
2. _____ prepares barbequed spare ribs.
3. _____ doesn't eat fried food.
4. _____ knows how to prepare stir fry.
5. _____ likes meat simmered in sauce.
6. _____ likes casseroles.
7. _____ likes food with chili powder.
8. _____ broils steak with seasoning.

DESSERTS

1. pastry	7. doughnut	13. cone	19. iced coffee	25. candy
2. brownie	8. pie	14. sundae	20. iced tea	_____
3. cake	9. pie ala mode	15. beverage	21. ice cream soda	_____
4. cheesecake	10. ice cream	16. coffee	22. milk shake	_____
5. cookies	11. frozen yogurt	17. cappuccino	23. lemonade	_____
6. coffee cake	12. sherbet	18. espresso	24. glass of water	_____

What's the Story?

Work in groups of five. • *Choose one table.* • *Write a story about the people.* • *Everyone in the group should contribute at least two sentences.* • *Read your story to the class.*

1. Who are the people?
2. Where are they?
3. What are they eating?
4. What is the children's favorite dessert?
5. What are the adults' favorite desserts?

Group Discussion

Work in groups of five. • Discuss these questions. • Report your answers to the class.

1. What is your favorite dessert?
2. Do you buy it or prepare it?
3. How do you prepare it?
4. Is it fattening?
5. How often do you have your favorite dessert?

INTERNATIONAL DESSERT MENU

Group Role Play

Work in groups of five. • First, fill in this menu with the desserts your group likes. • Decide on prices. • Then write a role play ordering dessert and coffee (or tea) at a coffee shop. • Present your role play to the class.

Cross-Cultural Exchange

Bring your favorite desserts or pastries to class • Take a break. • Have a dessert party • Taste everyone's dessert!

49

BREAKFAST

1. bacon	7. cream	13. home fries	19. oatmeal _____
2. bagel	8. cream cheese	14. jelly	20. orange juice _____
3. butter	9. danish	15. jam	21. pancakes _____
4. cereal	10. French toast	16. margarine	22. sugar _____
5. cereal bowl	11. (fried) egg	17. milk	23. syrup _____
6. cocoa	12. grits	18. muffin	24. toast _____

Partner Interview

Partner's name _____

Practice these questions with your teacher. • *Then ask your partner.*

1. What is a typical breakfast for you?
2. What time do you eat breakfast?
3. Do you eat breakfast with your family?
4. Do you eat breakfast at home?
5. In your opinion, what is a healthy breakfast?

50

Cross-Cultural Exchange

What do people usually eat for breakfast in your country? • *Tell the class.* • *Add new vocabulary to the list.*

Conversation Squares

Work in groups of three. • *First write your own answers.* • *Then ask your partners the questions.* • *Write their answers.* • *Compare your group answers with other groups.*

Breakfast	You _____	Partner 1_____	Partner 2_____
today	_____	_____	_____
yesterday	_____	_____	_____
tomorrow	_____	_____	_____

Group Survey

Ask everyone in your group these questions. • *Check ALWAYS, SOMETIMES, NEVER.* • *Count the answers.* • *Report your group results to the class.* • *Write the class results on the board.*

How often do you:	ALWAYS	SOMETIMES	NEVER
1. skip breakfast?	_____	_____	_____
2. drink coffee for breakfast?	_____	_____	_____
3. have cold cereal for breakfast?	_____	_____	_____
4. have hot cereal for breakfast?	_____	_____	_____
5. have fruit or fruit juice for breakfast?	_____	_____	_____
6. have something sweetfor breakfast?	_____	_____	_____
7. eat out for breakfast?	_____	_____	_____
8. eat a nutritious breakfast?	_____	_____	_____

LUNCH

1. bread	11. ketchup	21. roast beef	_____
2. brown paper bag	12. leftovers	22. salad	_____
3. bologna	13. lunchbox	23. salami	_____
4. cafeteria	14. lunchroom	24. sandwich	_____
5. cheese	15. mayonnaise	25. soup	_____
6. coffee mug	16. microwave oven	26. spaghetti	_____
7. cold cuts	17. mustard	27. spaghetti sauce	_____
8. frozen entree	18. peanut butter	28. thermos	_____
9. ham	19. plastic baggie	29. yogurt	_____
10. hero (submarine/grinder)	20. potato chips		_____

What's the Story?

Work in groups of five. • *Choose one scene and write a story.* • *Everyone in the group should contribute at least two sentences.* • *Read your story to the class.*

1. Where are the people?
2. What are their names?

3. What are they eating and drinking?
4. What are they saying?

Partner Interview

Practice these questions with your teacher. • *Then ask your partner.*

1. What time do you usually eat lunch?
2. Where do you eat lunch?
3. What do you usually eat for lunch?
4. What do you usually drink for lunch?
5. Do you usually eat a nutritious lunch?
6. Do you ever skip lunch? Why?
7. Do you bring your lunch to work?(to school?) What do you bring?
8. Do you make your own lunch? If not, who makes it for you?
9. If you buy your lunch, where do you buy it? How much does it cost?
10. Who do you usually eat lunch with? What do you talk about?

Write

What is your favorite sandwich? • *How do you prepare it?* • *Write the recipe.* • *Tell the class how to make your favorite sandwich.*

_____
(1)

Spread _____ on
(2)

_____ .
(3)

Put _____ on the bread
(4)
and close the sandwich.

Cut in half.
Enjoy the sandwich!

Choose one:

(1)   roast beef sandwich
      peanut butter & jelly
      tuna fish sandwich
      ham & cheese sandwich
      other:_____

(2)   mayonnaise
      butter
      margarine
      mustard
      ketchup
      peanut butter
      other:_____

(3)   rye bread
      white bread
      wheat bread
      a roll
      other:_____

(4)   roast beef
      tuna fish
      ham and cheese
      jelly
      other:_____

53

FAST FOOD

1. counter
2. line
3. customer
4. order
5. drive-in window
6. hamburger
7. bun
8. chicken nuggets
9. hot sauce (salsa)
10. salad dressing
11. pickle
12. salad bar
13. soda (pop)
14. shake
15. large
16. medium
17. small
18. straw

_____
_____
_____
_____
_____

Group Survey

Ask everyone in your group these questions. • *Check YES or NO.* • *Count the answers.* • *Report your group results to the class.* • *Write the class results on the board.*

Do you:	YES	NO
1. ever eat fast foods?	_____	_____
2. like hamburgers with everything?	_____	_____
3. like french fries?	_____	_____
4. like ketchup on your fries?	_____	_____
5. like pizza?	_____	_____
6. like hot dogs?	_____	_____
7. like mustard on your hot dogs?	_____	_____
8. like tacos?	_____	_____
9. like hot salsa?	_____	_____
10. think fast foods are bad for you?	_____	_____

Partner Role Play

With your partner, complete this role play. • *Present your role play to the class.*

Cashier: May I help you?
Customer: _____

Cashier: Anything to drink?
Customer: _____

Cashier: Anything else?
Customer: _____

Cashier: That'll be $ _____.__ please.

(Customer gives cashier $20.00. Cashier takes out change from the cash register. Gives back change)

Cashier: That's $_____ change. Have a nice day.

JUNK FOOD

1. vending machine	6. corn chip	11. popcorn	_____
2. bubble gum	7. cracker	12. pretzel	_____
3. candy bar	8. gum	13. soda	_____
4. cheese snack	9. juice drink	14. tortilla chip	_____
5. chocolate bar	10. peanut		_____

Class Discussion

1. Which junk foods do you like? Which don't you like?
2. Do you ever eat junk food? When?
3. Where do you buy junk food?

Class Game: *"What is your favorite junk food?"*

Write the name of your favorite junk food. • Fold your paper. • Make a pile. • Open one. • Guess who wrote the paper. • Who likes the same junk food?

Group Decision

Work in groups of five or six. • Your group has $5.00 to spend on snacks. • Look at the illustration • What will you buy from the machines? • Tell the class.

DINNER

1. restaurant	6. maitre d'	11. smoking section _____
2. waiter	7. cashier	12. rest rooms _____
3. waitress	8. check	13. drink _____
4. busboy	9. tip	14. beer _____
5. hostess	10. no smoking section	15. wine _____

What's the Story?

Work in groups of five. • *Choose one table and write a story.* • *Everyone in the group should contribute at least one sentence.* • *Read your story to the class.*

1. Who are the people? What are their names?
2. Why are they going out to eat tonight?
3. What are they having for dinner?
4. How are they feeling tonight?
5. What are they saying?
6. Who will pay the check?
7. What will they do after they leave the restaurant?

THE SUPERMARKET

1. bottle	5. aisle	9. bottle return	13. tomato paste
2. jar	6. shelf	10. can return	14. whipped cream
3. loaf	7. courtesy desk	11. section	15. grated cheese
4. dozen	8. checkout counter	12. rice	16. tomato sauce

Class Vocabulary Challenge

Write in as many labels as you can. • *Compare labels with others in the class.*

Group Decision

Work in groups of three or four. • *Compare these jars of tomato sauce.* • *Report your answers to the class.*

largest			
smallest			
most expensive			
cheapest			
best buy			

Community Activity

Review this list with your teacher. • *Add two items.* • *Go to your supermarket.* • *Fill out the chart.* • *In the next class, compare your charts.*

SUPERMARKET NAME:			
ITEM	**SIZE**	**BRAND NAME**	**PRICE**
1. Bread	_____	_____	_____
2. Coffee	_____	_____	_____
3. Rice	_____	_____	_____
4. _____	_____	_____	_____
5. _____	_____	_____	_____

REVIEW

Group Decision

Work in groups of five or six. • *Choose one of the family pictures.* • *Plan menus for one day (breakfast, lunch, dinner and snacks) for the family.* • *Figure the cost.*

Breakfast

$_____

Lunch

$_____

Dinner

$_____

Snacks

$_____

Class Game: *"What is it?"*

Choose a leader.

> **Leader:** Think of a food you like. Don't say it!
> **Class:** Ask the leader YES/NO questions.
> **Leader:** Answer "yes" or "no".
> > **Example:** Is it green?
> > Is it a vegetable?
> **Class:** Try to guess the food. Whoever guesses is the new leader.

International Party

Bring special foods from your country to class. • *Have an international party.* • *Bring tapes of music from your country to play at the party.* • *Enjoy!*

60

UNIT 5

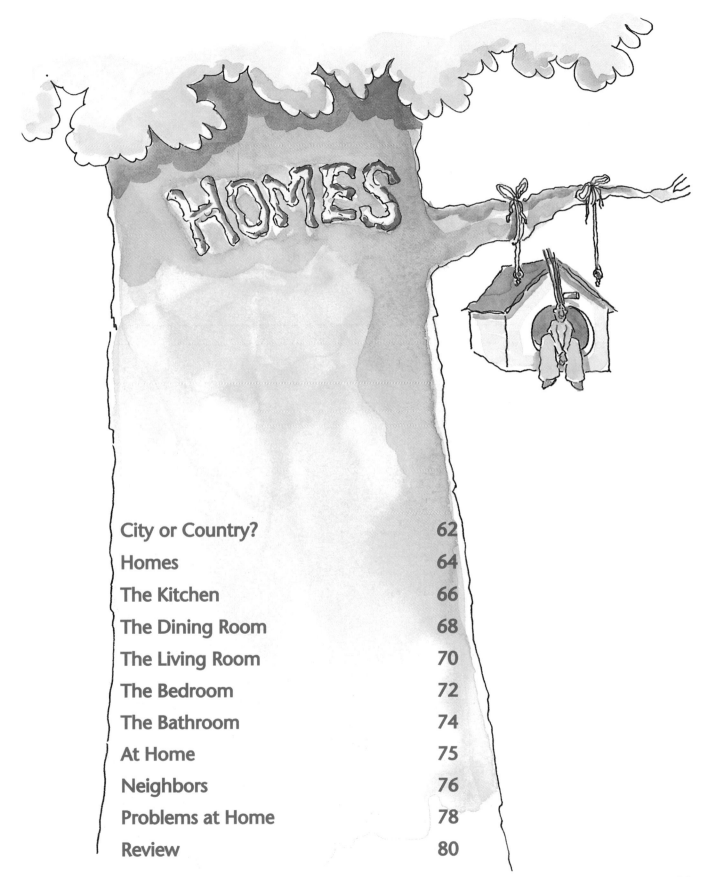

CITY OR COUNTRY?

1. coast	6. farm	11. busy	_____
2. desert	7. ranch	12. calm	_____
3. jungle	8. rural	13. crowded	_____
4. mountains	9. suburban	14. exciting	_____
5. noisy	10. country	15. peaceful	_____

Partner Interview

Partner's name _____

Practice these questions with your teacher. • *Then ask your partner.*

1. Where do you live now?
2. How long have you lived there?
3. Where were you born?
4. Where did you grow up?
5. Where do you want to live?

Group Discussion

Work in groups of three. • *Discuss these questions.* • *Report your answers to the class.*
1. Do you like where you live now?
2. In your opinion, where is the best place in the world to live?
3. Decide as a group which place you like best. Tell your class why. If you can't agree on a place, tell your class why you can't agree.

Speech

Bring in a picture or a photo of a beautiful place to live. • *Tell the class about the picture.* • *Use these questions as a guide.*
1. Where is the place?
2. Why do you think it is beautiful?
3. Why do you want to live there?

Group Game: "Gossip!"

Work in groups of eight. • *Choose a leader.* • *Close your books.* • *Look at the cover.* • *What are the people saying?*

Leader: (*To the first student*) Read the secret on page 197. Close your book. Whisper the secret to the student sitting next to you.

Next Student: Whisper the secret to the student sitting next to you, etc.

Last Student: Write the secret on the board or tell the class.

Class: Check the secret on page 197. Which group had the most accurate secret?

HOMES

1. home	9. attic	17. terrace	_____
2. house	10. balcony	18. roof	_____
3. apartment (flat)	11. basement	19. floor	_____
4. condominium	12. chimney	20. yard	_____
5. dormitory	13. fence	21. adobe	_____
6. mobile home	14. garage	22. brick	_____
7. motel	15. garden	23. cement	_____
8. prison	16. porch	24. wood	_____

What's the Story?

Work in groups of three. • Decide which home to describe. • Write a story about the home and the people. • Everyone in the group should contribute at least two sentences. • Read your story to the class.

64

Conversation Squares

First write your own answers. • *Then ask your partners the questions.* • *Write their answers.* • *Compare your group's answers with the other groups.* • *Make a class directory.*

1. **What's your name?**
First/Middle/Last: _____
What's your address?
Number/Street _____
Apartment number _____
City or Town _____
State _____ Zip code _____
What's your phone number?
Area Code: (_____)
Number: _____

3. **What's your name?**
First/Middle/Last: _____
What's your address?
Number/Street _____
Apartment number _____
City or Town _____
State _____ Zip code _____
What's your phone number?
Area Code: (_____)
Number: _____

2. **What's your name?**
First/Middle/Last: _____
What's your address?
Number/Street _____
Apartment number _____
City or Town _____
State _____ Zip code _____
What's your phone number?
Area Code: (_____)
Number: _____

4. **What's your name?**
First/Middle/Last: _____
What's your address?
Number/Street _____
Apartment number _____
City or Town _____
State _____ Zip code _____
What's your phone number?
Area Code: (_____)
Number: _____

THE KITCHEN

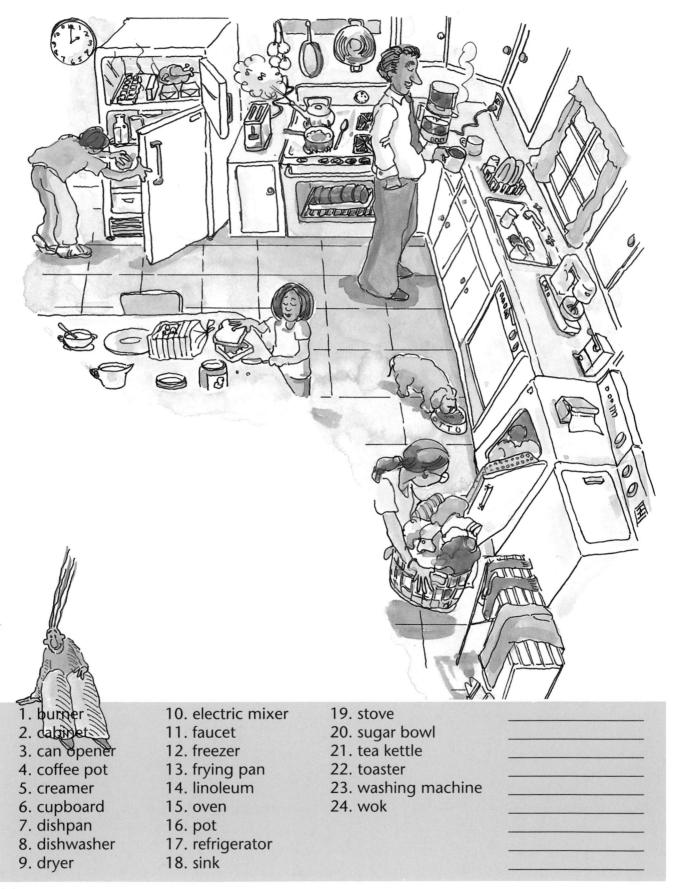

1. burner	10. electric mixer	19. stove
2. cabinet	11. faucet	20. sugar bowl
3. can opener	12. freezer	21. tea kettle
4. coffee pot	13. frying pan	22. toaster
5. creamer	14. linoleum	23. washing machine
6. cupboard	15. oven	24. wok
7. dishpan	16. pot	
8. dishwasher	17. refrigerator	
9. dryer	18. sink	

What's the Story?

Work in groups of five. • *Write a story about the kitchen.* • *Everyone in the group should contribute at least two sentences.* • *Read your story to the class.*

1. Where is the family?
2. What are their names?
3. What time is it?
4. What is the family doing?

Partner Game: *"Same or Different?"*   **Partner's name** _____

One partner looks at the picture on this page. • *The other partner looks at the picture on page 66.* • *Compare kitchens.* • *List everything in both kitchens.* • *What is the same?* • *What is different?*

67

THE DINING ROOM

1. set the table
2. plate
3. salad bowl
4. saucer
5. soup bowl
6. silverware
7. tablespoon
8. teaspoon
9. pie server
10. serving spoon
11. glass
12. napkin
13. pitcher
14. pepper shaker
15. salt shaker
16. tablecloth
17. candle stick
18. vase

_____
_____
_____
_____
_____

Partner Interview

Practice these questions with your teacher. • *Then ask your partner.*

1. What room do you eat in at home?
2. How do you set the table at home: for breakfast? lunch? dinner?
3. Does your family always eat together?

Group Activity

Work in groups of four or five. • *With your group, list five things people say at the dinner table.* • *Read your list to the class.* • *Make a list on the board.*

Group Role Play

Work in groups of five. • *Choose one scene.* • *Write a role play with your group.* • *Include roles for everyone.* • *Present your role play to the class.*

1. a family eating together
2. a family setting the table for dinner with guests.
3. a teenager eating with his (or her) friends in the kitchen.

Include in your role play:

1. the people (give them names!)
2. how they feel
3. what they are saying
4. what is on the table
5. the food

Cross-Cultural Exchange

What are some traditional eating customs in your country? • *Tell the class.* • *How are the customs the same in different countries?* • *Which countries are the most similar?*

THE LIVING ROOM

1. sofa (couch)	9. drapes	17 photograph _____
2. armchair	10. carpet	18. picture _____
3. throw pillow	11. stereo	19. plant _____
4. coffee table	12. cd player	20. relax _____
5. television (tv)	13. laser disk player	21. watch tv _____
6. VCR	14. radio	22. listen to music _____
7. lamp	15. speakers	23. nap _____
8. lampshade	16. bookcase	_____

Group Vocabulary Challenge

Work in groups of four. • Make a list of everything you do in your living rooms. • Read your list to the class. • Which group had the most new words? • Make a list on the board. • Copy the list into your notebook.

Class Game: *"What do you do in the living room?"*

Think. • Write an activity. • Fold your paper. • Make a pile of papers. • Open one. • Follow the instruction. • Ask "What am I doing?" • Have the class guess the activity.

Group Game: *"Gossip!"*

Work in groups of eight. • Choose a leader. • Close your books. • Look at the cover. • What are the people saying?

Leader: *(To the first student) Read the secret on page 197. Close your book. Whisper the secret to the student sitting next to you.*

Next Student: *Whisper the secret to the student sitting next to you, etc.*

Last Student: *Write the secret on the board or tell the class.*

Class: *Check the secret on page 197. Which group had the most accurate secret?*

Community Activity

Bring in flyers from stores that sell furniture. • Decide as a class how to furnish a living room. • What will you buy? • How much will each item cost? • What will the total bill be?

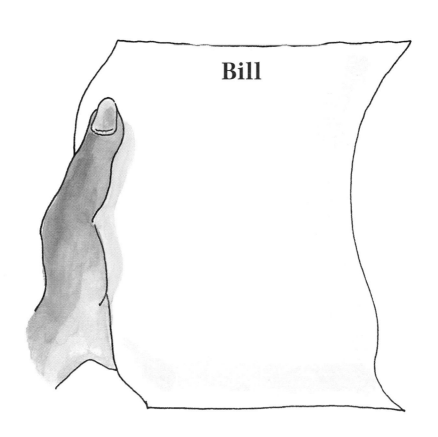

GOING SHOPPING!

1. coffee shop (cafe)	7. mall	13. sports shop	_____
2. department store	8. men's clothing store	14. stationery store	_____
3. electronics store	9. music store	15. toy store	_____
4. flower shop	10. pharmacy	16. women's clothing store	_____
5. hardware store	11. shoe store		_____
6. jewelry store	12. shopping center		_____

Class Activity

Are these stores in your neighborhood? • Write the names of your neighborhood stores on the signs. • What do you buy in each of the stores? • Make a list on the board of three items for each store.

Group Discussion

Work in groups of five. • Discuss these questions. • Report your answers to the class.

     1. Where do you shop?
     2. When do you go shopping?
     3. What stores do you go to?
     4. Which stores in your neighborhood do you like best? Why?
     5. Which store do you recommend to the class?

SPORTS STORE

1. baseball	7. fishing reel	13. golf tees	19. ski boots
2. baseball bat	8. fishing rod	14. helmet	20. skis
3. baseball glove	9. fly (flies)	15. hockey puck	21. ski poles
4. basket ball	10. football	16. hockey stick	22. soccer ball
5. bowling ball	11. golf ball	17. pads	23. soccer shoes
6. cleats	12. golf club	18. skates	24. sweatsuit

Class Discussion

1. What is your favorite sport?
2. Where do you buy sports equipment?
3. What do you buy?
4. Is it expensive? How much does it cost?
5. What kind of clothing do you buy in a sports store?

Group Decision

Work in groups of four. • *Decide what to buy for one of the following situations.* • *Report your decisions to the class.*

1. Your ten-year-old nephew is having a birthday. He is on a baseball team for the first time.
2. Your sister and brother-in-law are having an anniversary. Your sister likes to play golf. Your brother-in-law likes to bowl.
3. You live in a warm climate. You want to take up a new sport.

Group Vocabulary Challenge

Work in groups of four. • *Make a list of special equipment you need for these sports.* • *Read your list to the class.* • *Which group had the most new words?* • *Make list on the board.* • *Copy the list into your notebook.*

skiing	baseball
golf	hockey
ice skating	basketball
bowling	other: _____

Partner Activity

Partner's name _____

Match the items. • *Compare your answers with the class.*

A	**B**
ski poles	puck
soccer ball	baseball
hockey stick	bowling shoes
baseball glove	soccer shoes
bowling ball	ski jacket

TOY STORE

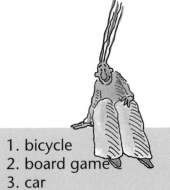

1. bicycle	6. electric train	11. rubber ball	16. truck
2. board game	7. fire engine	12. stuffed animal	_____
3. car	8. mobile	13. teddy bear	_____
4. computer game	9. model airplane	14. toy kitchen	_____
5. doll	10. paint set	15. tricycle	

Partner Activity

Practice these questions with your teacher. • *Then ask your partner.*

1. When you were a child, did you have a favorite toy? What was it?
2. What children's toys were popular in your country when you were a child? What is popular now?
3. What do children like to play with where you live now?
4. Do you buy toys? Where do you buy them?

Group Decision

Work in groups of four. • *Decide what toy to buy for each of these children.* • *Report your decisions to the class.*

1. a baby girl
2. a two-year-old boy
3. an eight-year-old boy
4. a five-year-old girl
5. a ten-year-old girl

Group Survey

Ask everyone in your group these questions. • *Check YES or NO.* • *Count the answers.* • *Report your group results to the class.* • *Write the class results on the board.*

When you were a child:	YES	NO
1. did you ever play with dolls?	_____	_____
2. did you ever play with marbles?	_____	_____
3. did you like to color?	_____	_____
4. did you like to play ball?	_____	_____
5. did you like to read?	_____	_____

DEPARTMENT STORE

1. appliances	7. elevator	13. women's department _____
2. children's department	8. escalator	14. men's department _____
3. cosmetics	9. gift wrap	15. men's room _____
4. customer service	10. home entertainment	16. store directory _____
5. domestics	11. home furnishings	17. ladies room _____
6. dressing room	12. jewelry counter	

Class Discussion

1. Is there a department store in your neighborhood? Where?
2. Do you shop there? What do you buy?
3. Which is your favorite department store? Why do you like it?
4. Are department stores the same or different in your country? Tell the class.

Partner Game: *"What do you remember?"*   Partner's name _____

*Look at the picture with your partner. • Remember as much as you can. • Close your book. •
Describe the picture. • List everything • Compare your notes with another pair of students. •
Add to your list.*

Partner Role Play   Partner's name _____

*With your partner, write role plays for three of these situations. • Present your role plays
to the class.*

You are at the escalator and want to get to:

1. the gift wrap counter
2. the children's department
3. the jewelry department
4. the returns counter
5. the men's department

FLORIST

1. bouquet	7. daisy	13. gladiola	19. philodendron _____
2. bud	8. fern	14. iris	20. pot _____
3. carnation	9. florist	15. leaf	21. ribbon bow _____
4. corsage	10. floral arrangement	16. lily	22. stem _____
5. crocus	11. gardenia	17. orchid	23. thorn _____
6. daffodil	12. geranium	18. petal	_____

What's the Story?

Work in groups of three or four. • *Tell the story of each person in the florist shop.* • *Everyone in the group should contribute at least two sentences.* • *Read your story to the class.*

1. Who are the people? What are their names?
2. What occasions are they buying flowers for?
3. What are they going to do when they leave the shop?

Group Role Play

Work in groups of three or four. • *Choose one situation.* • *Write a role play.* • *Include roles for everyone.* • *Present your conversation to the class.*

1. You are buying flowers for your 85-year-old grandmother's birthday. What do you buy? How much do you want to spend? What will you write on the card?
2. Your friend is in the hospital. You want to buy some flowers or a plant to bring when you visit. How much do you want to spend? What do you want to buy? What will you write on the card?
3. It's the last day of class. You are buying a plant for your teacher. How much money did you collect? What will you buy? Will you have the florist put a ribbon around the plant? What color? What will you write on the card?

Class Discussion

1. What is your favorite flower? Why do you like it?
2. When do you buy flowers?
3. Is there a florist in your neighborhood? Where? What can you buy?
4. How can you send flowers?
5. When do people give flowers and plants in your country?

PHARMACY

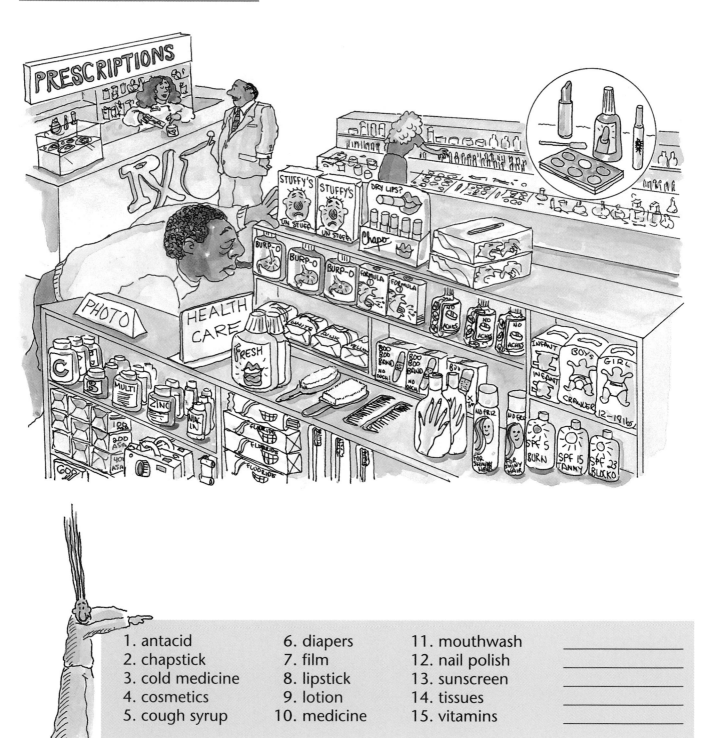

1. antacid	6. diapers	11. mouthwash	_____
2. chapstick	7. film	12. nail polish	_____
3. cold medicine	8. lipstick	13. sunscreen	_____
4. cosmetics	9. lotion	14. tissues	_____
5. cough syrup	10. medicine	15. vitamins	_____

Group Vocabulary Challenge

Work in groups of four or five. • *Make a list everything you buy at the pharmacy.* • *Compare your list with another group.* • *Which group had the most new words?* • *With the class, make a list of new words on the board.* • *Copy the list into your notebook.*

Class Poll

Take a poll. • Use the list on the board. • How many students buy the items at the pharmacy? • Write the total next to each item. • What do most students buy?

Conversation Squares

Work in groups of three. • First write your own answers. • Then ask your partners the questions. • Write their answers. • Compare your group answers with other groups.

Brand	You _____	Partner 1_____	Partner 2_____
	_____	_____	_____
	_____	_____	_____
	_____	_____	_____
	_____	_____	_____
	_____	_____	_____

Community Activity

Compare the prices for the following items in two different stores. • Report the results to the class.

ITEM	STORE:_____	STORE:_____
soap: brand _____		
size: _____	Price $_____	Price $_____
shampoo: brand_____		
size:_____	Price $_____	Price $_____
toothpaste: brand_____		
size:_____	Price $_____	Price $_____
Vitamin C: brand_____		
size_____	Price $_____	Price $_____
dose_____		
cough syrup: brand_____		
size_____	Price $_____	Price $_____

JEWELRY SHOP

1. bracelet	6. jade	11. ruby	_____
2. chain	7. necklace	12. turquoise	_____
3. diamond	8. pearl	13. wedding ring	_____
4. emerald	9. pin		_____
5. engagement ring	10. ring		_____

Group Role Play

Work in groups of five or six. • *Choose one pair of people in the jewelry store.* • *Write a role play.* • *Include roles for everyone.* • *Present your role play to the class.*

Partner Interview   Partner's name _____

Practice these questions with your teacher. • *Then ask your partner.*

1. Do you wear any jewelry? What do you wear?
2. What jewelry are you wearing today?
3. Do you ever buy jewelry? Who do you buy jewelry for?
4. Did you ever receive jewelry for a present? What did you get?

HARDWARE STORE

1. bolts	9. hatchet	17. plane	25. tool box
2. chisel	10. key	18. pliers	26. turpentine
3. crowbar	11. level	19. power saw	27. vise
4. electric drill	12. lock	20. sandpaper	28. washer
5. electrical tape	13. nuts	21. stepladder	29. wire
6. glue	14. paint	22. switch	30. wrench
7. glue gun	15. paintbrush	23. tape measure	
8. handsaw	16. paint can	24. tool	

Class Discussion

1. Do you ever go to the hardware store?
2. Which one?
3. What do you buy?
4. How are the prices?

Partner Activity

Partner's name _____

Decide what is happening in the picture. • *Report your answers to the class:*

1. What is the man going to do with the ladder?
2. Why is the woman making a duplicate key?
3. What is the woman buying at the cash register?
4. What will the couple use the paint for? What color will they choose?

Class Game: *"Mime"*

Pantomime using a tool. • *Whoever guesses the tool takes the next turn.*

OFFICE SUPPLY STORE

1. card
2. computer paper
3. correction fluid
4. desk calendar
5. envelope
6. file cabinet
7. manila folder
8. masking tape
9. paper clip
10. rubber band
11. rubber cement
12. stapler
13. staples
14. tape
15. typing paper
16. typewriter ribbon

_____
_____
_____
_____
_____

Class Discussion

What do you use these supplies for?

Find Someone Who

Review the vocabulary with your teacher. • *Fill in the name of someone who . . .*

1. _____ can type.
2. _____ can change a typewriter ribbon.
3. _____ can use a fax machine.
4. _____ has a desk calendar.
5. _____ can use a copy machine.

Group Activity

Work in groups of four or five. • *Put the supplies you have with you on the desk.* • *Make a list of what your group has.* • *Compare your list with the class.*

ELECTRONICS STORE

1. adding machine	10. CD (compact disk)	19. monitor
2. answering machine	11. color television	20. personal computer
3. audio cassettes	12. computer keyboard	21. printer
4. black & white TV	13. cordless phone	22. short wave radio
5. boombox	14. fax machine	23. tape deck
6. calculator	15. floppy disk	24. telephone cord
7. camcorder	16. headphones	25. telephone jack
8. car radio	17. modem	26. turntable
9. cassette recorder	18. modular telephone	27. videotape

Group Decision

Work in groups of five or six. • *Decide on the best prices for the items in the illustration.* • *Write price tags.* • *Compare your prices with the class.*

Class Discussion

1. What electronic equipment do you have?
2. What do you want?
3. What equipment do you like to use?
4. Do you use any of this equipment at work? What do you use?
5. What kind of equipment is popular in your country? What do people have in their homes?

SALES AND ADVERTISEMENTS

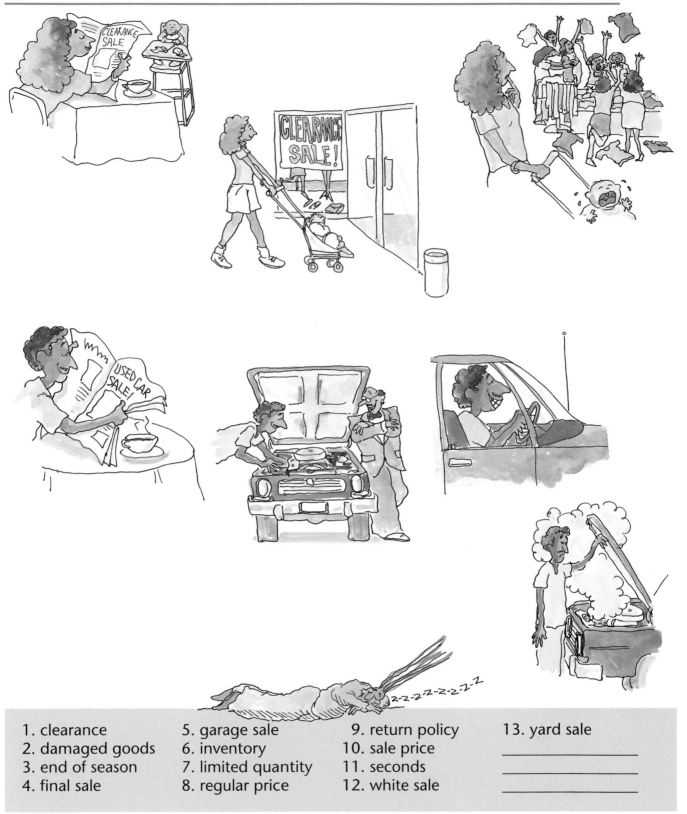

1. clearance	5. garage sale	9. return policy	13. yard sale
2. damaged goods	6. inventory	10. sale price	_____
3. end of season	7. limited quantity	11. seconds	_____
4. final sale	8. regular price	12. white sale	_____

Class Activity

Tell the stories. • *Did you ever have an experience like this?* • *Tell the class about your experience.*

Group Discussion

Work in groups of five.   •   Discuss these questions.   •   Report your answers to the class.
    1. Do you like to shop at sales?
    2. What did you buy on a sale?
    3. Is there a good sale now? Where?
    4. What store in your community has the best sale?
    5. When do you have to be careful when you buy on sale?

Community Activity

Bring in flyers for sales to class.   •   What do you want to buy?   •   How much money can you save?

REVIEW

Group Decision

Work in groups of five. • Your group has $1000. • Decide how to spend it. • You can do something together or divide it. • If you divide it, each person decides how to spend his/her portion. • Report your decisions to the class. • Remember to tell:

1. what you will buy
2. where you will buy it
3. who you will buy it for
4. when you will buy it
5. what you will do with it

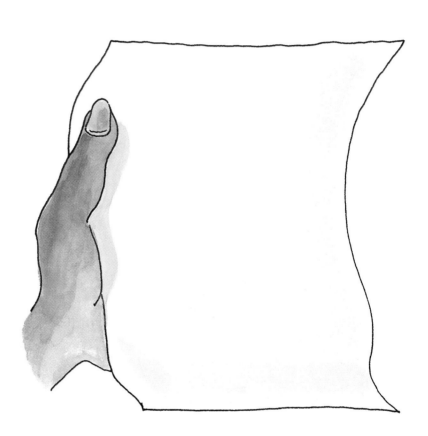

Partner Writing Activity   Partner's name _____

Ask your partner these questions. • Then write a paragraph about your partner. • Read your paragraph to your partner. • Read it to the class.

1. Is money important to you? Why?
2. Do you ever save money?
3. What do you like to spend money on?
4. What don't you like to spend money on?
5. If you won the lottery, what would you do with the money?

Speech

Tell the class about your favorite store. • Include everything you like about the store. • Show the class something you bought there.

UNIT 7

YOUR NEIGHBORHOOD

1. convenience store	7. parking meter	13. stoop
2. ice cream truck	8. parking space	14. street corner
3. laundromat	9. pizza shop	15. traffic
4. mailbox	10. recycling bin	16. traffic light
5. neighbor	11. shoemaker	17. trash can
6. newspaper store	12. stickball	18. urban

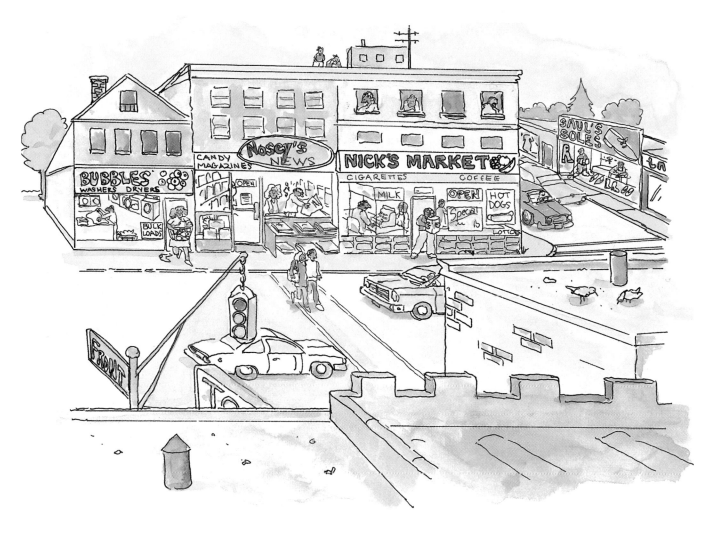

Class Discussion

1. Do you like your neighborhood? How long have you been living there?
2. Is there a traffic light on your street? Where is it?
3. Does the ice cream truck come to your neighborhood? When?
4. Do children play in the street in your neighborhood? What do they play?
5. Where do people walk their dogs in your neighborhood?

Find Someone Who

Review the vocabulary with your teacher. Fill in the name of someone who . . .

1. _____ lives near a playground.
2. _____ lives near a mailbox.
3. _____ lives near a store.
4. _____ recycles paper.
5. _____ recycles can and bottles.

YOUR COMMUNITY

1. bank	10. school	19. in front of
2. church	11. supermarket	20. just before
3. city hall	12. bus	21. just past
4. hospital	13. subway	22. next to
5. library	14. taxi	23. on the corner
6. movie theater	15. train	24. straight ahead
7. parking lot	16. across from	25. turn right (left)
8. post office	17. behind	26. (two) blocks
9. public phone	18. between	27. opposite

Class Discussion

1. Does your city look like this? What buildings do you recognize?
2. Do you go to the library? Does the library have a foreign book section? What languages ? Do you have a library card?
3. When do you go to the post office? What do you ask for? Do you ever have problems there?
4. Is there a bank in your community? Do you use it? When? What do you do there?
5. Is there public transportation in your community? Is it good? Do you use it? When do you use it?

Partner Role Play   Partner's name _____

Complete these conversations. • Use the map on page 108. • Present your conversations to the class.

1. **At City Hall**
   A: Excuse me. How can I get to the post office?

   B: _____

   A: Thank you.

2. **At the Bank**
   A: Excuse me. Can you tell me how to get to the library?

   B: _____

   A: Thanks.

3. **At the Movie Theater**
   A: Pardon me. Could you please tell me where I can park my car?

   B. _____

   A: Thanks very much.

4. **At the Drug Store**
   A: Pardon me. Do you know where I can make a phone call?

   B: _____

   A: Thanks a lot.

5. **At the Subway Station**
   A: Say. Can you tell me where the school is?

   B: _____

   A: Thank you.

THE TELEPHONE

1. answering machine	7. hold	13. rotary dial	_____
2. busy signal	8. local call	14. telephone call	_____
3. cord	9. long distance	15. telephone number	_____
4. cordless	10. message	16. touch tone	_____
5. directory assistance	11. operator (assisted)	17. wrong number	_____
6. hang up	12. receiver	18. 800 number	_____

Class Discussion

What is happening in these pictures?

Partner Interview

Partner's name _____

Practice these words with your teacher. • *Then ask your partner.*

1. What is your telephone number?
2. What is your area code?
3. What kind of telephone do you have?
4. Do you make a lot of long distance calls? Where do you call?
5. Who do you call most often?

Cross-Cultural Exchange

What are telephones like in your country? • *How do you make a long distance call?* • *Do many people have telephones in their homes?*

110

Partner Role Play

Complete these phone conversations. • *Present one to the class.*

1. **Answering machine**

   Machine: I'm not here right now. Please leave a message at the tone. BEEEEEP

   You:_____

2. **Wrong number**

   Stranger: Hello.

   You: Hello. This is_____. Is_____ there?

   Stranger: _____

   You: _____

3. **Long distance directory assistance**

   Operator: What city?

   You: _____

   You: I'd like the number for_____

   Operator: Please hold for the number:

   (or) The number is: _____

Partner Role Play

Decide what to say for these phone calls. • *Present one to the class.*

1. local directory assistance for the number of your school
2. your school when you can't come to class
3. the landlord when your roof is leaking
4. the drug store when you need to know their hours
5. the telephone company when your bill is incorrect

Community Activity

Use your local telephone directory. • *Find the names, addresses and telephone numbers.*

LOOK UP	ADDRESS	TELEPHONE NUMBER
1. a drug store _____	_____	_____
2. a movie theater_____	_____	_____
3. a restaurant _____	_____	_____
4. a plumber _____	_____	_____
5. a church _____	_____	_____
6. your school _____	_____	_____
7. your hospital _____	_____	_____
8. the telephone company business office _____	_____	_____
9. local directory assistance _____	_____	_____
10. long distance directory assistance _____	_____	_____

EMERGENCY: FIRE!

1. ambulance	6. fire fighter	11. smoke
2. ax	7. fire hydrant	12. stretcher
3. burn	8. hook	13. victim
4. EMT	9. hose	
5. fire escape	10. siren	

Class Discussion

What is happening in the picture? • What do you think caused the fire? • How can fires be prevented?

What's the Story?

Work in groups of four. • *Choose one person in the picture.* • *Tell that person's story.* • *Everyone in the group should contribute at least one sentence.* • *Read your story to the class.*

    1. What is his/her name?
    2. Why is he/she at the fire scene?
    3. What is he/she doing?
    4. What will happen next?

Group Discussion

Work in groups of four. • *Discuss these questions.* • *Report your answers to the class.*

    1. Have you ever seen a fire? What happened?
    2. Are you afraid of fire? Why or why not?
    3. Did you play with fire when you were a child? What did you do?
    4. Are fires a problem in your country? Why or why not?
    5. Tell the most interesting story to the class.

Group Role Play

Work in groups of four. • *Write a role play.* • *Include roles for everyone.* • *Present your conversation to the class.*

    1. Where is the fire?
    2. How did it start?
    3. Where are you?
    4. What do you do?

Partner Role Play   Partner's name _____

Write a conversation to report a fire to the 911 emergency operator. • *Present your conversation to the class.*

911 Operator: _____

You: _____

911 Operator: _____

You: _____

911 Operator: _____

You: _____

EMERGENCY: POLICE!

1. arrest
2. break
3. break in
4. carjack
5. crime
6. danger
7. freeze!
8. handcuffs
9. hubcap
10. Miranda rights
11. owner
12. police
13. police car
14. report
15. steal
16. thief
17. witness

_____
_____
_____
_____
_____
_____

Strip Story

What is happening? • *Fill in the bubbles.*

Group Decision

Work in groups of four. • *What should you do in these emergencies?* • *Decide with your group.*
• *Report your decisions to the class.*

Partner Activity

Partner's name _____

Choose one emergency. • *Write a conversation between the 911 operator and yourself.* •
Present your conversation to the class.

1. Who are you?
2. Where are you?
3. What happened?
4. When did it happen?
5. Is anyone hurt?
6. What should you do while you wait?

THE POST OFFICE

1. air mail	7. mail	13. postal worker
2. counter	8. mail truck	14. scale
3. envelope	9. overnight mail	15. stamp
4. first class	10. package	16. stamp machine
5. insurance	11. parcel post	17. third class
6. letter	12. post card	18. two-day delivery

Class Discussion

What is happening in the picture?

Class Game: *"What do you remember?"*

Look at the picture. • Remember as much as you can. • Close your book. • List everything. • Compare your answers with your class. • Who had the longest list? • Open your book and check your answers.

Partner Activity

Partner's name_____

Choose a person from the line in the picture. • *Write a paragraph and read it to the class.*

1. What is the person's name?
2. What is he/she doing at the post office?
3. What will he/she say when it is his/her turn?
4. Where is the letter or package going?
5. Who will receive it?

Partner Role Play

Partner's name_____

Write a conversation for you and a postal clerk. • *Present your conversation to the class.*

1. What do you want at the post office?
2. What will the clerk say to you?
3. What will you say to the clerk?
4. How much money will you need?

Partner Interview

Partner's name_____

Practice these questions with your teacher. • *Then ask your partner.*

1. Do you like to write letters?
2. How often do you write letters?
3. Who do you write to?
4. How often do you receive letters?
5. How often do you go to the post office?
6. What do you do there?

Group Problem Posing/Problem Solving

Work in groups of three. • *State the problem.* • *Find a solution.* • *Report your decisions to the class.*

You wait on line for ten minutes in the post office. You buy stamps and some post cards for $12.80. You give the clerk a $50.00 bill. The clerk gives you $7.20 in change.

THE BANK

1. account	8. credit card	16. PIN number
2. ATM	9. deposit slip	(personal
(automated teller	10. loan application	identification)
machine)	11. money order	17. safety deposit box
3. bank	12. monthly statement	18. save
4. bank officer	13. overdraw	19. savings account
5. cash	14. payroll check	20. teller
6. change	15. personal check	21. travellers' check
7. checking account		22. withdrawal slip

Class Activity

What are the people doing in the bank? • *Make a list on the board of everything they are doing.*

Class Discussion

1. What is the name of the closest bank to your home? Where is it?
2. Do you use the bank?
3. When do you go to the bank?
4. Do you have a savings account? a checking account?
5. What are some things you can put in the safety deposit box?

Group Problem Posing/Problem Solving

Work in groups of three. • *State the problems.* • *Find solutions.* • *Report your decisions to the class.* • *Present a role play about one of these problems.*

This woman works in a bank. She's a teller. You are cashing a check for $50 and she gives you $60. What do you say? What will she do?

This man is a bank robber. He is robbing the bank. What will the teller do? What will the robber do? What should you do if you are there?

This man overdrew his account. What will he do? What should you do if you overdaw your account.

PUBLIC TRANSPORTATION

1. bus stop	7. fare	13. passenger	19. token
2. cab	8. front	14. platform	20. transfer
3. driver	9. front door	15. rear	21. turnstile
4. entrance	10. get off	16. rear door	22. wait
5. exact change	11. get on	17. seat	
6. exit	12. metro	18. taxi driver	

Class Discussion

1. What kind of public transportation do you have in your community?
2. Do you use it? When?
3. How much is the bus fare? The subway fare?
4. Is it crowded? When is it most crowded?
5. Do you get on at the front or in the rear? Where do you get off?
6. What do you say if you want to get off?
7. Is it safe? When is it dangerous? Why is it dangerous?

Group Role Play

Work in groups of three. • *Write a conversation between the taxi driver and the two riders.* • *Include roles for everyone.* • *Present your conversation to the class.*

Group Problem Posing/Problem Solving

Work in groups of three. • *State the problems.* • *Find solutions.* • *Report your decisions to the class.*

1. You take the bus to school on the first day of class. After two stops, you realize you are on the wrong bus.
2. You are in a subway station with two friends, waiting for the train. The train comes. You get on, but the door closes too fast. Your friends are still on the station.
3. You get on the bus. After the bus starts, you realize you don't have exact change.

Group Survey

Ask everyone in your group these questions. • *Check the kinds of transportation and advantages.* • *Count your answers.* • *Report your group results to the class.* • *Write the class results on the board.*

What transportation do you use?	Cheap	ADVANTAGES		
		Convenient	Fast	Safe
bus				
train				
taxi				
private car				
bicycle				
feet				

YOUR CAR

1. accelerator(gas pedal)	11. fuel gauge	21. seat belt	_____
2. baby seat	12. gas cap	22. signal light	_____
3. brake	13. gear shift	23. speedometer	_____
4. bumper	14. glove compartment	24. steering wheel	_____
5. car key	15. hood	25. temperature gauge	_____
6. clutch	16. hub cap	26. tail light	_____
7. emergency brake	17. ignition	27. trunk	_____
8. exhaust pipe	18. license plate	28. wheel	_____
9. headlight	19. odometer	29. windshield	_____
10. fender	20. rear view mirror	30. windshield wiper	_____

Partner Interview

Partner's name _____

Practice these questions with your teacher. • *Then ask your partner.*

1. Do you have a driver's license?
2. Do you drive a standard shift? an automatic?
3. Do you have a car? What kind?
4. What kind of car would you like to drive?
5. What is the most popular car in your country?

TRAFFIC AND ROAD SIGNS

Class Discussion

1. Have you ever seen any of these signs? Which ones?
2. What should you do:
   - at a Railroad Crossing sign?
   - at a Yield sign?
   - at a Speed Limit sign?
   - at a School Zone sign?

Community Activity

Which of these signs are in your neighborhood? • *What color is each sign?* • *Draw the signs in your neighborhood.* • *Note the colors.* • *Bring your signs to class.* • *What do they say?* • *What do the colors signify?*

THE GAS STATION

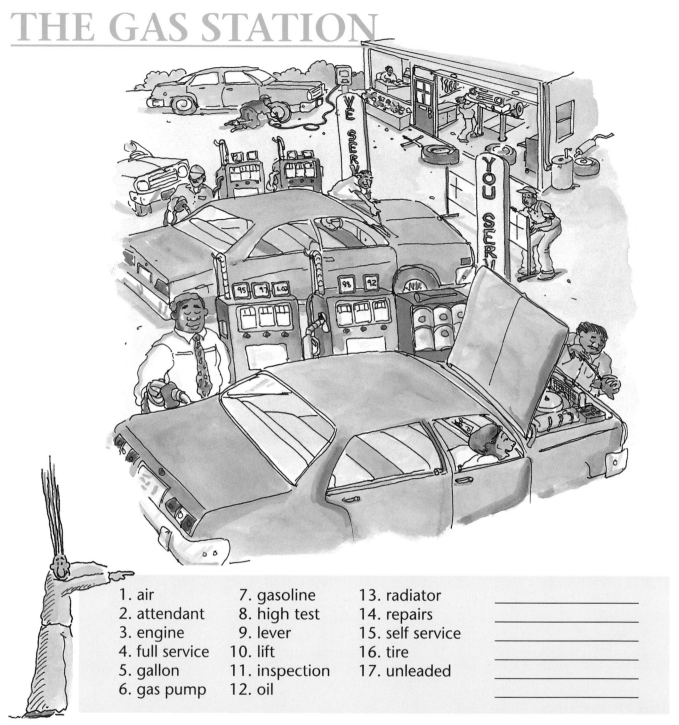

1. air	7. gasoline	13. radiator	_____
2. attendant	8. high test	14. repairs	_____
3. engine	9. lever	15. self service	_____
4. full service	10. lift	16. tire	_____
5. gallon	11. inspection	17. unleaded	_____
6. gas pump	12. oil		_____

Partner Activity

Partner's name _____

Decide what to say. • *Present your answers to the class.*
1. you want the attendant to check your oil
2. you want $10 worth of super unleaded gasoline
3. you have a flat tire and need some help
4. you need your car inspected

Group Vocabulary Challenge

Work in groups of four or five. • *Close your books.* • *Write a list of vocabulary words about cars and gas stations.* • *Compare your list with another group.* • *Which group had the most new words?* • *With the class, make a list on the board.* • *Copy the new words into your notebook.*

124

THE LAUNDROMAT & DRY CLEANERS

1. bleach	6. dirty	11. press	16. starch
2. clean	7. dry cleaner	12. rinse cycle	17. warm water
3. cold water	8. hot water	13. sort	18. wash cycle
4. dark wash	9. hanger	14. spin cycle	19. washing machine
5. detergent	10. load	15. spot	20. white wash

Partner Game: *"What do you remember?"*   Partner's name _____

Look at the picture. • Remember as much as you can. • Close your book. • Describe the picture with your partner. • List everything. • Compare your list with another pair of partners. • Add to your list.

What's the Story?

Work in groups of five. • Write a story about the scene in the laundromat. • Everyone in the group should contribute at least two sentences. • Use these questions or make up your own • Read your story to the class.

1. Who are the people?
2. What are their names?
3. What day is it?
4. What time is it?
5. What will happen between the man and the woman?

REVIEW

Speech

Choose a topic and explain it to the class:

1. How do you ride a bus?
2. How do you get gas at a self-service station?
3. How do you wash clothes at the laundromat?
4. How do you call directory assistance?
5. How do you buy stamps at the post office?
6. How do you report a fire emergency?

Partner Vocabulary Challenge

Partner's name _____

Make lists to answer each question. • *Read your list to the class.*

1. What do people do at the bank?
2. What do people do at the post office?
3. What emergencies do people call 911 for?
4. What do people do at the gas station?
5. What do people do at the dry cleaners?

Community Activity

Draw a map from your school to your house. • *Explain your map to your class.*

UNIT 8

WORK

WORK EVERYONE DOES!

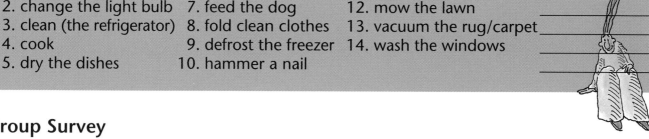

1. burned out	6. dust the furniture	11. iron clothes _____
2. change the light bulb	7. feed the dog	12. mow the lawn _____
3. clean (the refrigerator)	8. fold clean clothes	13. vacuum the rug/carpet _____
4. cook	9. defrost the freezer	14. wash the windows _____
5. dry the dishes	10. hammer a nail	_____

Group Survey

Ask everyone in your group these questions. • *Check EVERY DAY/OFTEN/OCCASIONALLY/NEVER.*
• *Count your answers.* • *Report your group results to the class.* • *Write the class results on the board.*

How often do you:	EVERY DAY	OFTEN	OCCASIONALLY	NEVER
cook?	_____	_____	_____	_____
change a light bulb?	_____	_____	_____	_____
wash the dishes?	_____	_____	_____	_____
hammer a nail?	_____	_____	_____	_____
paint the house?	_____	_____	_____	_____
dust the furniture?	_____	_____	_____	_____
mow the lawn?	_____	_____	_____	_____

Class Game: *"Test your memory"*

Practice the vocabulary with your teacher. • Close your book. • Listen to your teacher tell the story. • Open your book. • Write the correct order. • Read your story to the class in the correct order.

Cross-Cultural Exchange

Who does the housework in your home? • In your country, do men help with housework? • Should men help with housework? • Why/why not? • What electric appliances do people use to do housework in your country?

HOME REPAIRS

1. batteries	7. hinge	13. sew	_____
2. board	8. material/cloth	14. sewing machine	_____
3. circuit breaker	9. needle	15. scissors	_____
4. flashlight	10. putty	16. screw	_____
5. fuse	11. putty knife	17. screwdriver	_____
6. fuse box	12. saw	18. thread	_____

Class Activity

Make a list on the board of work you can do with each of the tools. • Copy the list into your notebook.

Group Decision

Work in groups of five. • Decide what to do for each situation. • Report your decisions to the class.

1. The sink is clogged in the bathroom.
2. Your daughter dropped a gold ring down the toilet.
3. The lights went out in the house.
4. There is a small hole in the wall of the living room.
5. A shelf fell down from the wall.

What's the Story?

Work in groups of five. • *Choose one of the pictures and write a story.* • *Everyone in the group should contribute at least two sentences.* • *Read your story to the class.*

Answer these questions:

1. Who?
2. What?
3. Where?
4. When?
5. Why?

JOBS

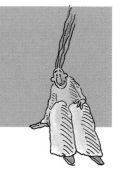

1. barber	6. factory worker	11. secretary	_____
2. carpenter	7. farm worker	12. teacher aide	_____
3. construction worker	8. fisherman	13. full time	_____
4. chef	9. manicurist	14. part time	_____
5. engineer	10. mechanic		_____

Class Discussion

Where do these people work? • What do they do?

Group Activity

Work in groups of five. • Fill in the chart with your group. • Compare your answers with another group. • Report your answers to the class.

WHO?	WHAT?	WHERE?
farm worker	picks crops	on a farm
teacher	teaches	in a school
factory worker	_____	_____
cook	_____	_____
manicurist	_____	_____
healthcare worker	_____	_____
secretary	_____	_____
barber	_____	_____
hospital aide	_____	_____
mechanic	_____	_____
salesperson	_____	_____
security guard	_____	_____
taxi driver	_____	_____

Group Activity

Work in groups of five. • *Decide with your group what jobs these people have.* • *For question five, decide on a job.* • *Draw a picture.* • *Write the job title.* • *Report your decision to the class.*

1._____

2._____

3._____

4._____

5._____

Partner Role Play

Partner's name _____

A TV host is interviewing you. • *Choose a job.* • *Write a conversation between the TV host and yourself.* • *Present your role play to the class.*

1. Where do you work?
2. What is your job?
3. What hours do you work?

4. Do you like your job?
5. What job do you want in the future?

CLOTHING FOR WORK

JOB	CLOTHING/EQUIPMENT	
1. astronaut	9. badge	_____
2. ballet dancer	10. gun	_____
3. butcher	11. lab coat	_____
4. custodian	12. night stick	_____
5. lifeguard	13. space suit	_____
6. nurse	14. uniform	_____
7. police officer	15. whistle	_____
8. lab technician	16. work clothes	_____

Class Discussion

1. What work do these people do?
2. Why do they wear uniforms or costumes?
3. Who pays for the uniforms?
4. Which uniforms do you like? Why?
5. Which uniforms require special shoes? special hats? special gloves?

Group Discussion

Work in groups of four. • *Look at the pictures.* • *Discuss these questions.* • *Report your opinions to the class.*

1. What are the people wearing?
2. What are their jobs?

3. Are they dressed appropriately?
4. What do you wear to work?

Cross-Cultural Exchange

In your country, do uniforms and costumes look like this? • *Which are the same?* • *Which are different?*

SAFETY AT WORK

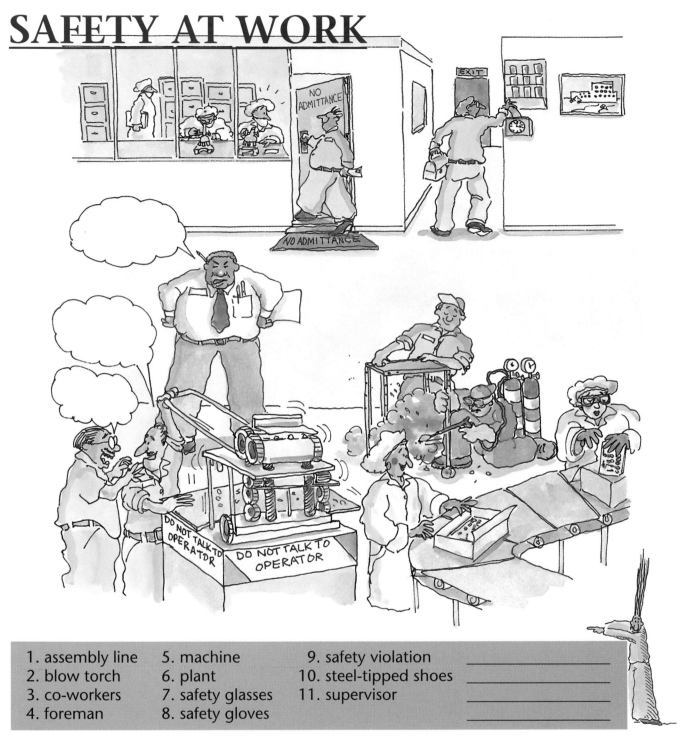

1. assembly line	5. machine	9. safety violation
2. blow torch	6. plant	10. steel-tipped shoes
3. co-workers	7. safety glasses	11. supervisor
4. foreman	8. safety gloves	

Class Discussion

1. What is happening in this picture?
2. What jobs do the people have?
3. Do you think anyone is a supervisor? Which one(s)?
4. Are there any safety violations in the factory? What are the violations?
5. What kind of factory do you think it is?

Group Decision

Work in groups of five. • *Decide what the people are saying.* • *Fill in the bubbles.* • *Compare your bubbles with the class.*

136

Class Discussion

What do these signs mean? • Where do you see these signs?

Group Role Play

Work in groups of four or five. • Choose one of these situations. • Write a role play. • Include roles for everyone. • Present your conversation to the class.

1. You are new on the job. Several of you do the same job. You are unsure of what to do. Ask your coworkers. When no one knows for sure, check with your supervisor.
2. It's Friday afternoon. You are taking a break. Several coworkers are sitting in the lounge having coffee and snacks. Have a conversation.

Community Activity

Are there any signs in the school building? • What do they say? • Do you notice any signs at your job? • Copy them and bring them to class. • Look for signs in other buildings. • Copy the signs. • Show the signs to the class. • Who can guess where the sign is from?

WORKING ON A FARM

1. barn	7. calf	13. foal	19. ram	25. piglet
2. barnyard	8. rooster	14. duck	20. ewe	_____
3. corral	9. hen	15. duckling	21. lamb	_____
4. silo	10. chick	16. goose	22. pig	_____
5. bull	11. stallion	17. gosling	23. boar	_____
6. cow	12. mare	18. sheep	24. sow	_____

Cross-Cultural Exchange

What do these animals "say" in your native language? • *Fill in the chart*

ANIMAL	ENGLISH	YOUR LANGUAGE
cat	meow	_____
dog	bow wow	_____
cow	moo	_____
rooster	cock a doodle doo	_____
hen	cluck cluck	_____
horse	neigh	_____
pig	oink	_____
duck	quack	_____

1. bucket	5. milking machine	9. pitchfork	13. trough	_____
2. clippers	6. hay	10. rope	14. wool	_____
3. field	7. orchard	11. shear		_____
4. gather eggs	8. pick apples	12. tractor		_____

Class Discussion

What is happening in these pictures? • What other work do people do on farms and ranches?

Partner Activity

Partner's name _____

Which word doesn't belong? • *Cross out the word.* • *Report your answers to the class.*

1.	sheep	wool	clipper	goggles
2.	barn	milk	saw	cow
3.	orchard	iron	crop	harvest
4.	pitchfork	grass	hay	dog
5.	trough	saddle	eggs	horse
6.	ladder	hatchet	bucket	rooster
7.	gather	shear	pick	saddle

PROBLEMS AT WORK

1. appropriate	5. employee	9. overwork	_____
2. boss	6. employer	10. personal problem	_____
3. company time	7. excuse	11. (sexual) harassment	_____
4. discrimination	8. lazy	12. understanding	_____

Class Discussion

What is happening in each of these pictures? • Discuss the problems together.

Group Problem Posing/Problem Solving

Work in groups of four. • State the problems. • Pick one problem. • Find a solution. • Role play the problem and the solution for the class.

Conversation Squares

First write your own answers • Then ask your partners the questions. • Write their answers. • Compare your group answers with other groups.

Problem	You_____	Partner 1_____	Partner 2_____
What was it?	_____	_____	_____
How long did it last?	_____	_____	_____
What was the solution?	_____	_____	_____
Who helped you?	_____	_____	_____

LOSING YOUR JOB

1. close down	5. manager	9. quit	13. unemployed
2. destroy	6. migrant work	10. seasonal work	_____
3. fire	7. out of work	11. slow down	_____
4. lay off	8. poor performance	12. temporary	_____

Partner Activity

Partner's name _____

Look at the pictures. • *Decide what is happening.* • *Write captions for each story.* • *Tell the stories to the class.*

Find Someone Who

Review the vocabulary with your teacher. • *Fill in the name of someone who . . .*

1. _____ has been laid off.
2. _____ has quit a job.
3. _____ has kept a bad job.
4. _____ has left a good job.
5. _____ has had seasonal work.

142

Group Activity

Work in groups of three. • *Answer these questions.* • *Compare your answers with others in the class.*

1. What are good reasons to quit a job?

   _____

   _____

   _____

2. What are good reasons to keep a job?

   _____

   _____

   _____

3. What are good reasons to fire an employee?

   _____

   _____

   _____

FINDING A JOB

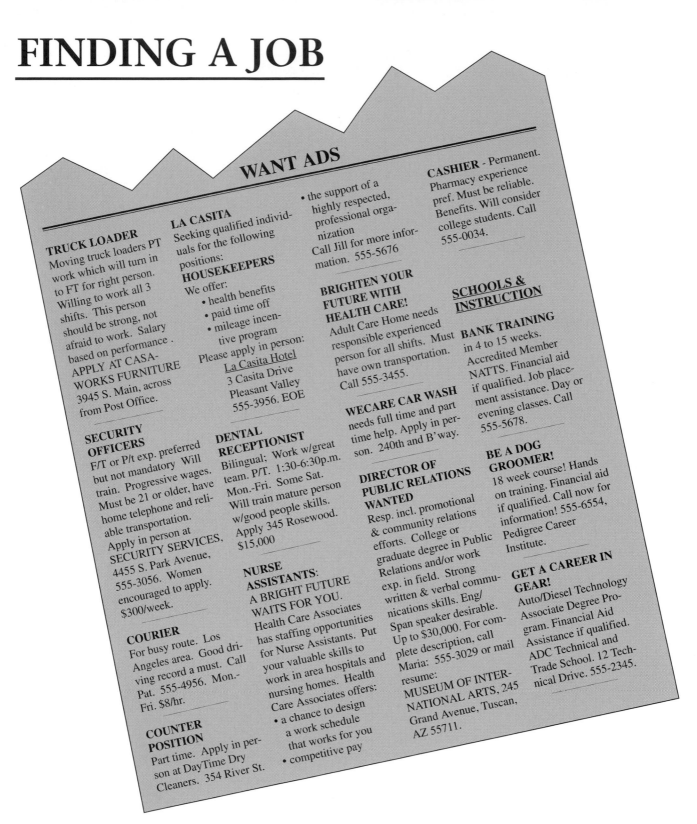

WANT ADS

TRUCK LOADER
Moving truck loaders PT work which will turn in to FT for right person. Willing to work all 3 shifts. This person should be strong, not afraid to work. Salary based on performance. APPLY AT CASA-WORKS FURNITURE 3945 S. Main, across from Post Office.

SECURITY OFFICERS
F/T or P/t exp. preferred but not mandatory Will train. Progressive wages. Must be 21 or older, have home telephone and reliable transportation. Apply in person at SECURITY SERVICES, 4455 S. Park Avenue, 555-3056. Women encouraged to apply. $300/week.

COURIER
For busy route. Los Angeles area. Good driving record a must. Call Pat. 555-4956. Mon.-Fri. $8/hr.

COUNTER POSITION
Part time. Apply in person at DayTime Dry Cleaners. 354 River St.

LA CASITA
Seeking qualified individuals for the following positions:
HOUSEKEEPERS
We offer:
• health benefits
• paid time off
• mileage incentive program
Please apply in person:
La Casita Hotel
3 Casita Drive
Pleasant Valley
555-3956. EOE

DENTAL RECEPTIONIST
Bilingual; Work w/great team. P/T. 1:30-6:30p.m. Mon.-Fri. Some Sat. Will train mature person w/good people skills. Apply 345 Rosewood. $15,000

NURSE ASSISTANTS:
A BRIGHT FUTURE WAITS FOR YOU. Health Care Associates has staffing opportunities for Nurse Assistants. Put your valuable skills to work in area hospitals and nursing homes. Health Care Associates offers:
• a chance to design a work schedule that works for you
• competitive pay

• the support of a highly respected, professional organization
Call Jill for more information. 555-5676

BRIGHTEN YOUR FUTURE WITH HEALTH CARE!
Adult Care Home needs responsible experienced person for all shifts. Must have own transportation. Call 555-3455.

WECARE CAR WASH
needs full time and part time help. Apply in person. 240th and B'way.

DIRECTOR OF PUBLIC RELATIONS WANTED
Resp. incl. promotional & community relations efforts. College or graduate degree in Public Relations and/or work exp. in field. Strong written & verbal communications skills. Eng/ Span speaker desirable. Up to $30,000. For complete description, call Maria: 555-3029 or mail resume:
MUSEUM OF INTER-NATIONAL ARTS, 245 Grand Avenue, Tuscan, AZ 55711.

CASHIER - Permanent. Pharmacy experience pref. Must be reliable. Benefits. Will consider college students. Call 555-0034.

SCHOOLS & INSTRUCTION

BANK TRAINING
in 4 to 15 weeks. Accredited Member NATTS. Financial aid if qualified. Job placement assistance. Day or evening classes. Call 555-5678.

BE A DOG GROOMER!
18 week course! Hands on training. Financial aid if qualified. Call now for information! 555-6554, Pedigree Career Institute.

GET A CAREER IN GEAR!
Auto/Diesel Technology Associate Degree Program. Financial Aid Assistance if qualified. ADC Technical and Trade School. 12 Technical Drive. 555-2345.

Class Discussion

1. Where do you think these ads are from? Have you ever seen ads like these?
2. Did you ever apply for a job through a newspaper ad? When? What kind of job was it?
3. What information do you look for in an ad?
4. When do you apply for a job through an ad?
5. Which one of these jobs in the newspaper ads interests you? Why?

Write

Fill out this employment application. • *Use it in the role play below.*

Date: _____ _____ _____
     (Month   )   (Day)   (Year)

Name: _____
     (First)   (Middle Initial)   (Last)

Social Security Number: _____

Address: _____
     (Number)   (Street)   (Apartment)

_____
     (City)   (State)   Zip Code)

Telephone:_____
     (Area Code)

Job Applying For:_____

Work Experience:_____

_____

_____

_____

_____

Education:_____

_____

_____

_____

Partner Role Play

Partner's name _____

Choose a job from the ads. • *One partner is the applicant.* • *One is the interviewer.* • *Present your rconversation to the class.*

Applicant: *ask some of these questions (or others):*
1. "What are the responsibilities of the job?"
2. "What are the hours?"
3. "Do I have to wear a uniform? Does the company provide the uniform?"
4. "What is the salary?"
5. "What are the company benefits? What am I eligible for?"

Interviewer: *ask some of these questions:*
1. "Why are you interested in this job?"
2. "Why are you thinking of leaving your present job?"
3. "Do you have any experience for this job?"
4. "Can you read and write English?"
5. "Can you work overtime?"

BENEFITS

1. disability
2. family leave
3. health insurance
4. hospitalization
5. paid holidays
6. pension
7. retirement
8. sick day
9. unemployment
10. vacation
11. workman's compensation

_____
_____
_____
_____
_____
_____

Class Discussion

Which of these benefits are most important to you? • Which benefits do you have in your present job?

146

Group Discussion

Work in groups of five or six. • *Discuss these questions.* • *Report your answers to the class.*
1. When do you take a sick day?
2. What do you do on your vacation?
3. What days are paid holidays?
4. When do you get hospital benefits?
5. What do you want to do when you retire?
6. What is "family leave?"
7. When does a worker qualify for worker's compensation?

Group Vocabulary Challenge

Work in groups of five or six. • *Make a list of the reasons to take a sick day.* • *Read your list to the class.* • *Which group had the most new words?* • *With the class, make a list of new words on the board.* • *Copy the list into your notebook.*

Class Game: *"What do you want to do on your next vacation?"*

Think. • *Write.* • *Fold.* • *Make a pile of papers.* • *Choose one.* • *Guess who wrote it.*

Group Problem Posing/Problem Solving

Work in groups of five or six. • *State this man's problem in one or two sentences.* • *Find a solution.* • *Compare your decisions with another group.*

Cross-Cultural Exchange

What benefits do employees usually get in your country? • *What is deducted from employees' paychecks?*

REVIEW

Ask your partner.

1. Where do you work?
2. What is your job?
3. What do you wear to work?
4. Do you work part time or full time?
5. When do you work?

Partner's name _____

6. Do you like your job?
7. Why or why not?
8. What is your boss like?
9. What do you want in the future?

Write

Write about your job.

I work at _____. My

(1)

job is _____. I wear _____ to

(2)   (3)

work. I work _____ and I work _____.

(4)   (5)

I _____ my job because it _____.

(6)   (7)

My boss is _____.

(8)

Someday, I want to work as _____.

(9)

Tell Your Partner

Read your journal entry to your partner. • *Listen to your partner's journal.*

UNIT 9

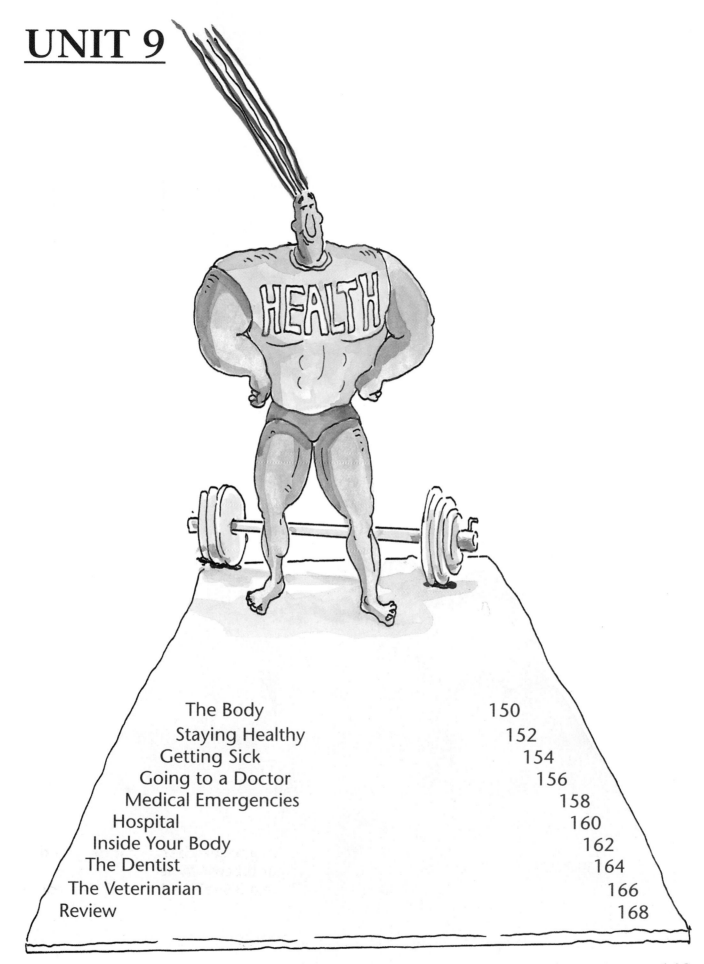

THE BODY

1. ankle	8. chin	15. forehead	22. leg	29. thigh
2. arm	9. ear	16. hand	23. lip	30. thumb
3. back	10. elbow	17. head	24. mouth	31. toe
4. buttock	11. eye	18. heel	25. neck	32. tooth
5. calf	12. face	19. hip	26. nose	33. waist
6. cheek	13. finger	20. jaw	27. shin	34. wrist
7. chest	14. fingernail	21. knee	28. shoulder	

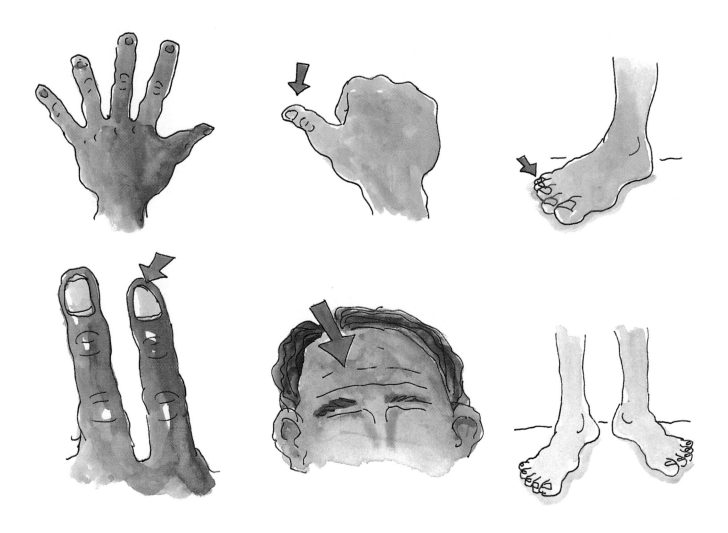

Group Game: *"What is it?"*

Work in groups of six. • Choose a leader.
> ***Leader:*** *Think about a part of the body. • Don't say what it is.*
> **Group:** *Ask the leader YES/NO questions.*
> ***Leader:*** *Answer "Yes" or "No".*
> **Group:** *Try to guess the word. Whoever guesses is the new leader.*

Class Game: *"Follow the Leader"*

Practice these instructions with your teacher. • Close your book. • Listen to your teacher. • Follow the instructions.
1. Stand up.
2. Nod your head (yes).
3. Shake your head (no).
4. Raise your left hand.
5. Touch your toes.
6. Put your hands on your hips.
7. Bend to the right.
8. Sit down.

STAYING HEALTHY

1. AIDS test
2. blood pressure
3. blood test
4. check up
5. cholesterol check
6. eye examination
7. height
8. measure
9. needle (syringe)
10. pregnancy check up
11. urine sample
12. vaccination
13. weigh
14. weight

_____
_____
_____
_____
_____

Class Discussion

What is happening in these pictures? • Are there clinics in your community? • Which ones?

Community Activity

Look in the telephone directory for the number of the Board of Health or your community hospital.
• List questions you want to ask on the board. • Call the number to find the answers.

Group Activity

Work in groups of five. • *How can you stay healthy?* • *Everyone in the group should contribute one answer to each question.* • *Compare your answers with the rest of the class.*

What is a nutritious meal?

Student's name	Advice

What is the best kind of exercise ?

Student's name	Advice

How many hours of sleep do you need each night?

Student's name	Advice

153

GETTING SICK

1. allergies	6. fever	11. nauseous	_____
2. backache	7. flu	12. sore throat	_____
3. cough	8. headache	13. stiff neck	_____
4. dizzy	9. indigestion	14. stomachache	_____
5. earache	10. laryngitis	15. toothache	_____

Class Discussion

1. What's wrong with these people?
2. How do you treat these common problems?
3. When do you go to the doctor for these problems?

Cross-Cultural Exchange

How do people in your country treat these problems?

Group Game: "What's the matter?"

Work in groups of four or five. • *Pantomime one of these problems for your group.* • *No speaking!* • *Whoever guesses takes the next turn.*

Partner Activity

Partner's name _____

Decide what medicines are in this cabinet. • *Fill in the labels.* • *On the empty bottle, write something from YOUR medicine cabinet.* • *Compare your answers with the class.*

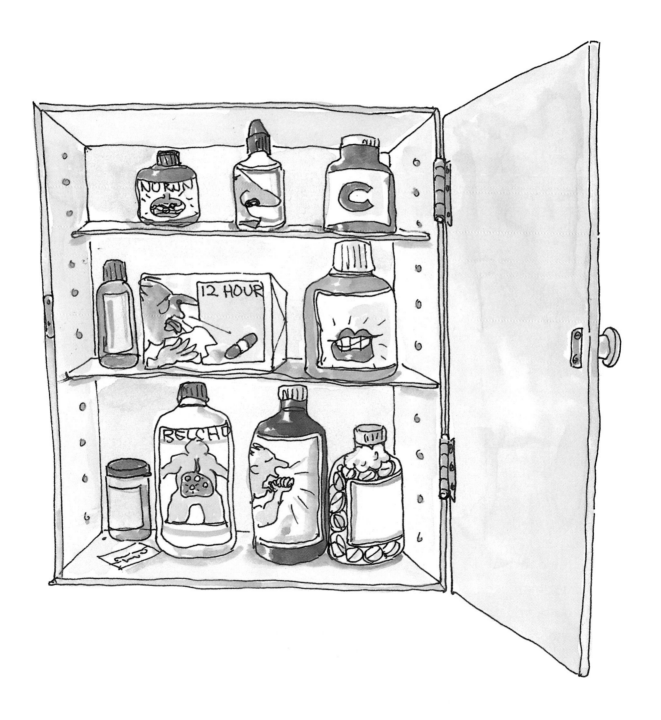

GOING TO A DOCTOR

➤ALLERGY

ALLERGY & IMMUNOLOGY ASSOCIATES
Arnold, Allan, M.D.
 326 North Ave., Oldtown.......................555-8070
Wykowski, Carla, M.D.
 4048 E. Wilson Dr., Newtown...............555-7890

➤CARDIOLOGY

Cassidy, James A., M.D.
 57 Park Ave., Oldtown.........................555-7895
 If No Answer Call.................................555-8382

➤DERMATOLOGY

Natale, Ellen, M.D.
 2123 S. Main St., Oldtown...................555-3024

➤EAR, NOSE & THROAT

Wu, Peter M., M.D.
 467 Valley View, Newtown............... 555-7974

➤FAMILY PRACTICE

NEWTOWN FAMILY CARE ASSOCIATES
 230 Valley View, Newtown
 New Patients Welcome
 Clinics..555-0682
 Garcia, Ana, M...................................555-9188
 St. Clair, Paul, M.D............................555-3025

➤GENERAL PRACTICE

Henry, Richard, D.O.
 2441 River St., Oldtown................... 555-6017
Johnson, Margaret, M.D.
General & Family Practice
 94 W. Wilson Dr., Newtown..................555-2198

➤INTERNAL MEDICINE

Hossaini, Ali, M.D.
Internal Medicine-Family Practice
 212 N. Main St., Oldtown......................555-9744

➤NEUROLOGY

UNIVERSITY PHYSICIANS CENTER
Brigham, Peter, M.D.
Papas, Irene, M.D.
 Toll Free.......................................1-800-555-7654
 501 Valley View, Newtown....................555-2341

➤OBSTETRICS/GYNECOLOGY

BIRTH AND WOMEN'S HEALTH CENTER
 376 River St., Oldtown.................... 555-7391

➤ONCOLOGY

OLDTOWN CANCER CENTER
 127 North Ave., Oldtown........................555-6090
 Cancer Helpline..........................1-800-555-HELP

➤OPHTHAMOLOGY

VALLEY EYE & LASER
Kaplan, Joan, M.D.
Harris, John, M.D.
 350 E. Wilson Dr., Newtown.................555-2135

➤PEDIATRICS

Rivera, Gloria, M.D.
 417 North Ave., Oldtown.......................555-3338

➤PSYCHIATRY

Bassu, Sadru, M.D.
 Board Certified
 438 Park Ave., Suite 6, Oldtown............555-5974

➤PULMONOLOGY

Kehrberg, Hartha, M.D.
 617 Valley View, Newtown....................555-3019

➤RADIOLOGY

Jorgensen, Eric, M.D.
 127 North Ave., Oldtown.......................555-6095

Group Decision

Work in groups of five or six. • Decide which doctor you need. • Report your decisions to the class.

1. You have rash and your skin is itchy. _____

2. You get headaches when you read. _____

3. You think you are pregnant. _____

4. You sneeze a lot when you are outdoors. _____

5. Your baby has a fever and won't eat. _____

6. You need a medical check-up as a requirement for your health insurance. _____

Partner Role Play

Partner's name _____

Make an appointment to see one of the doctors you listed above. • *One partner is the patient.* • *The other is the secretary or answering service.* • *Write a role play.* • *Present your role play to the class.*

> ***Patient:*** *ask these questions (or others):*
>> "When can I see the doctor?"
>> "What do I need to bring?"
>> "Do I have to pay at the visit or can the doctor bill me?"

> ***Secretary:*** *ask these questions (or others):*
>> "Have you ever seen the doctor before?" (If not, "Who recommended the doctor?")
>> "Do you have insurance? Which kind?"

Write

Fill out this form.

PATIENT INFORMATION FORM

Name: _____

Address: _____

_____

Phone number: _____

Insurance: YES _____   NO _____

Name of Insurer: _____

Medical Problem: (describe) _____

_____

How long have you had this problem? _____

Is it the result of an accident: YES _____   NO _____

(Describe accident) _____

Do you have a fever? YES _____   NO _____

Do you have pain?: YES _____   NO _____

Where? _____

Partner Role Play

Partner's name _____

You are visiting the doctor for the first time. • *One partner is the doctor.* • *The other is the patient.* • *Write a role play* • *Use the* PATIENT INFORMATION FORM. • *Present your role play to the class.*

MEDICAL EMERGENCIES

1. accident	6. fall	11. pulse
2. cast	7. heart attack	12. stitches
3. concussion	8. ice pack	13. stomach pump
4. EKG (electrocardiogram)	9. oxygen	14. stroke
5. emergency room	10. poison	15. x-ray

Class Discussion

Tell the stories together as a class. • What would you do in these situations? • Who has had a medical emergency? • Tell the class what happened.

Partner Activity

Partner's name _____

Decide what to do in these emergencies. • Report your answers to the class.

1. If someone next to you in the bus faints, what do you do?
2. If a person falls down a flight of stairs, what do you do?
3. If you cut yourself badly with a knife, what do you do?
4. If you step on a rusty nail, what do you do?
5. If you accidentally take poison, what do you do?

Group Decision

Work in groups of five. • Decide what supplies to use for each of the following emergencies.
• Report your decisions to the class.

bee sting   broken arm   splinter
sprained ankle   gash

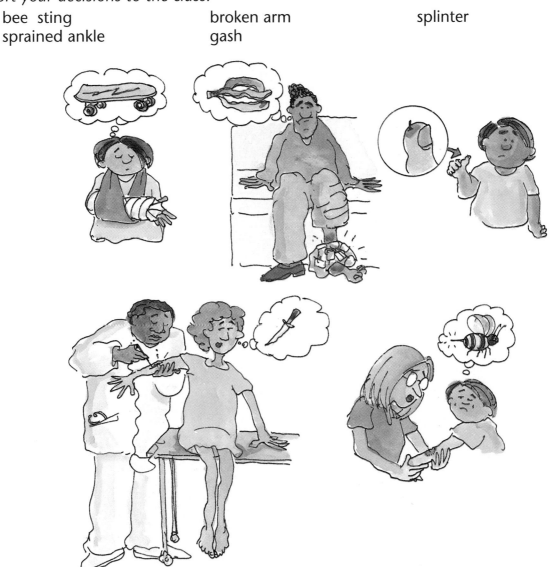

Community Activity

Answer these questions with your class. • Find out the missing information and report to the class.

1. What is the name of the closest hospital in your neighborhood?
2. Does the hospital have an emergency room? Where is it?
3. Did you ever go to the emergency room? Why?
4. Does your insurance cover emergency room visits?
5. What number do you call for emergencies?

HOSPITAL

1. blood transfusion	7. intensive care unit (ICU)	13. semi-private	_____
2. broken leg	8. intravenous (IV)	14. unconscious	_____
3. coma	9. nurse's station	15. visiting hours	_____
4. get well card	10. orderly	16. visitor	_____
5. hospital bed	11. patient		_____
6. information desk	12. private		_____

What's the Story?

Work in groups of five. • *Write a story about the hospital scene.* • *Everyone in the group should contribute at least two sentences.* • *Read your story to the class.*

1. Who are the people in this picture?
2. Who is sick? What is wrong?
3. What is the nurse doing?
4. What is the patient in room 208 doing? in room 209?
5. Who are the visitors? What room are they going to visit?

Hospital Signs

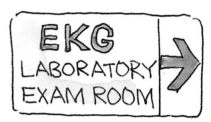

Partner Activity

Partner's name _____

Decide which sign to follow. • *Report your answers to the class.*

1. You want to buy a gift for your friend. _____
2. You are hungry and want to get some lunch after your visit. _____
3. You need to get a chest x-ray. _____
4. Your sister is having a baby and you need a place to wait. _____
5. You have to have a blood test. _____

INSIDE YOUR BODY

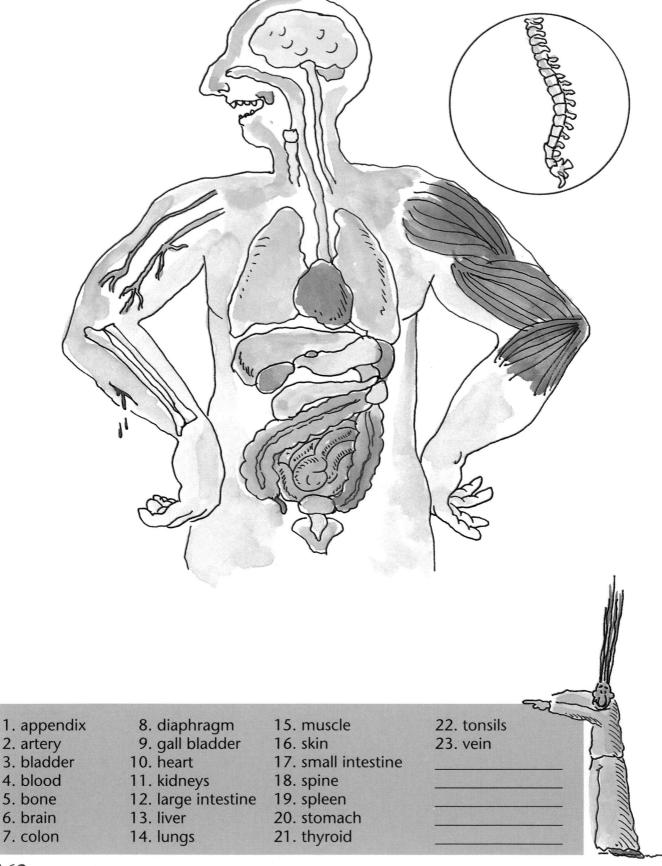

1. appendix
2. artery
3. bladder
4. blood
5. bone
6. brain
7. colon
8. diaphragm
9. gall bladder
10. heart
11. kidneys
12. large intestine
13. liver
14. lungs
15. muscle
16. skin
17. small intestine
18. spine
19. spleen
20. stomach
21. thyroid
22. tonsils
23. vein
_____
_____
_____
_____
_____

Group Activity

Work in groups of five or six. • *Decide on the part of the body where the problem is.* • *Compare your answers with the class.*

MEDICAL PROBLEM	PART OF THE BODY
1. heart attack	heart
2. tonsillitis	
3. lung cancer	
4. kidney infection	
5. gall stones	
6. appendicitis	
7. broken arm	
8. stroke	
9. tuberculosis	
10. other _____	

Cross-Cultural Exchange

Compare the treatments for these problems in different countries. • *Which treatments do you prefer?*

Group Game: *Gossip!*

Work in groups of eight. • *Choose a leader.* • *Close your books.* • *What are the people saying?*

Leader: (To the first student) Read the secret on page 203. Close your book. Whisper the secret to the student sitting next to you.

Next Student: Whisper the secret to the student sitting next to you, etc.

Last Student: Write the secret on the board or tell the class.

Class: Check the secret on page 203. Which group had the most accurate secret?

THE DENTIST

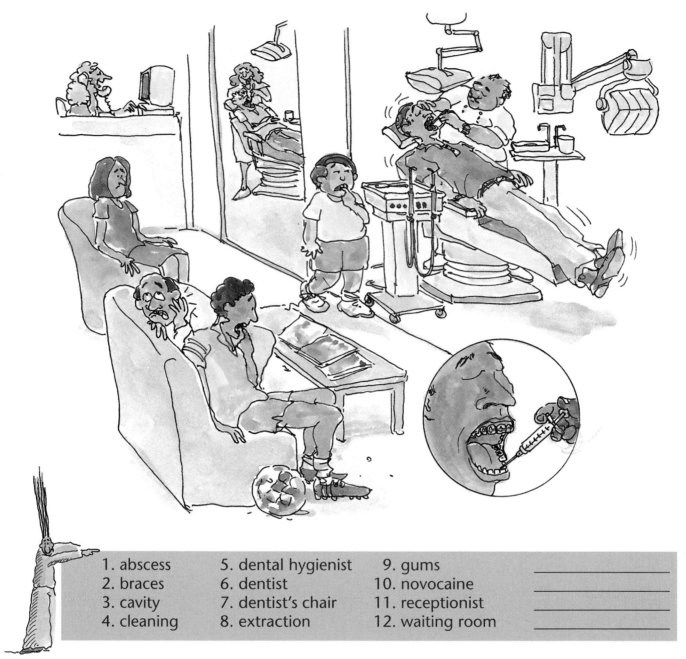

1. abscess	5. dental hygienist	9. gums	_____
2. braces	6. dentist	10. novocaine	_____
3. cavity	7. dentist's chair	11. receptionist	_____
4. cleaning	8. extraction	12. waiting room	_____

Partner Interview   Partner's name _____

Practice these questions with your teacher. • *Then ask your partner.*

1. Do you go to the dentist? What is your dentist's name?
2. Where is your dentist's office?
3. Do you like your dentist? Why or why not?
4. Did you ever have a toothache? What did you do?
5. Did you ever wear braces? When?
6. Did you ever have a filling? Did it hurt? Did you have novocaine?

Cross-Cultural Exchange

In your country, when do people go to the dentist? • *What kinds of fillings do people get?*

Partner Role Play

You have a toothache and can't eat. • Write a role play. • Make a telephone call for an appointment with the dentist. • Present your role play to the class.

What's the Story?

Work in groups of five. • Write a story for one of the patients in this picture. • Everyone in the group must contribute at least two sentences. • Read your story to the class. • Answer these questions:

1. What is the patient's name?
2. How old is she/he?
3. Why is this patient at the dentist's office?
4. How does she/he feel? Why?
5. How often does she/he visit the dentist?

6. Will she/he have novocaine?
7. What will the dentist (or the hygienist) do?
8. Does she/he like the dentist? Why or why not?
9. How will the patient feel when she/he leaves the office?
10. Where will she/he go?

Cross-Cultural Exchange

In some cultures, the "Tooth Fairy" takes children's baby teeth from under their pillows and leaves money. • Is there a special custom in your country for baby teeth? • Tell the class.

165

THE VETERINARIAN

1. assistant
2. board
3. cage
4. carrying case
5. examining table
6. inoculation
7. leash
8. license
9. rabies tag
10. veterinarian

_____
_____
_____
_____

What's the Story?

Work in groups of five or six. • Pick a pet in the picture. • Write a story. • Everyone in the group should contribute at least one sentence. • Read your story to the class. • Answer these questions:

1. What is the pet's name?
2. How old is it?
3. Why is the pet at the vet's?

4. What will the owner tell the vet?
5. What will the vet tell the owner?
6. What will the owner and the pet do after the visit?

Class Discussion

1. Do you have a pet? What kind?
2. What is your pet's name?
3. What kind of pet did you have as a child?
4. What kind of pet would you like to have? Why?
6. In your country, do people like to have pets? What are the most popular pets in your country?
7. What are some names for pets in your country?
8. Why do people take their pets to the vet?
9. Who is the best vet in your neighborhood?

Group Problem Posing/Problem Solving

Work in groups of three or four. • *Choose a situation.* • *State the problem.* • *Find a solution.* • *Report your decision to the class.*

Speech

Tell the class about pets in your country. • *Use these questions as a guide.*

1. Do many people have pets?
2. What are the most popular pets?
3. What are popular names for pets?

REVIEW

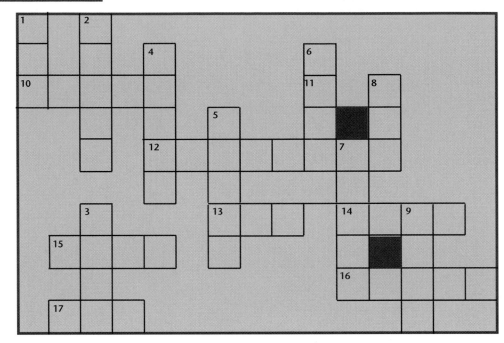

Write

Fill in this crossword puzzle. • *Check your answers with your partner.*

ACROSS

10.
11.
12.
13.

14.
15.
16.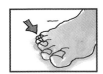
17.

DOWN

1.
2.
3.
4.

5.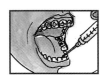
6.
7.
8.
9.

UNIT 10

LEISURE

LEISURE TIME

1. go camping	5. go to the movies	9. play the guitar	_____
2. go swimming	6. jog	10. play with a pet	_____
3. go to a baseball game	7. play dominoes	11. take photographs	_____
4. go to a party	8. play soccer	12. travel	_____

Group Vocabulary Challenge

Work in groups of five or six. • *Make a list of leisure time activities.* • *Read your list to the class.*
• *The group with the most activities is the winner!*

170

Group Survey

Ask everyone in your group these questions. • *Check SOMETIMES or NEVER.* • *Count the answers.* • *Report your group results to the class.* • *Write the class results on the board.*

In your leisure time, do you	SOMETIMES	NEVER
1. watch tv?	_____	_____
2. go to the movies?	_____	_____
3. read?	_____	_____
4. play with a pet?	_____	_____
5. listen to music?	_____	_____
6. play a musical instrument?	_____	_____
7. watch sports?	_____	_____
8. play a sport?	_____	_____
9. travel?	_____	_____
10. go camping?	_____	_____
11. go to school?	_____	_____

Partner Interview

Partner 's name _____

Practice these questions with your teacher. • *Then ask your partner.*

1. When do you have leisure time?
2. What do you like to do most in your leisure time?
3. What do you like to do on a rainy day?
4. What do you like to do in the summer?
5. What will you do on your next holiday?

What's the Story?

Work in groups of five. • *Write a story for the picture.* • *Everyone in the group should contribute at least one sentence.* • *Read your story to the class.*

GOING OUT

1. amusement park	5. dance	9. host	13. painting
2. club	6. dressed up	10. museum	14. roller coaster
3. concert	7. friend	11. musician	15. sculpture
4. cotton candy	8. guest	12. opera	16. singer

Class Discussion

With your class, decide on captions for each picture.

172

Find Someone Who

What do you like to do when you go out? • *Review the vocabulary with your teacher.* • *Fill in the name of someone who . . .*

1. _____ likes to ride a roller coaster.
2. _____ goes to church every week.
3. _____ likes to visit museums.
4. _____ likes to go to parties.
5. _____ likes to go dancing.
6. _____ likes to go to concerts.
7. _____ goes out with friends every day.
8. _____ has gone to an opera.
9. _____ likes to go to the movies.
10. _____ likes to stay home.

Partner Role Play   Partner's Name _____

Write a telephone conversation. • *One partner invites the other to do something.* • *Present your conversation to the class.*

Community Activity

Bring a local newspaper to class. • *Look in the ENTERTAINMENT section.* • *Are there any interesting events?* • *How much do they cost?* • *Plan a class field trip.* • *Enjoy!*

WATCHING TELEVISION

1. cable	6. game show	11. soap opera	_____
2. cartoons	7. late night show	12. talk show	_____
3. channel	8. mystery	13. variety show	_____
4. comedy	9. program		_____
5. commercial	10. sad		_____

What's the Story?

Work in groups of five. • Write a story about the picture. • Everyone in the group should contribute one line. • Read your story to the class. • Who had the funniest story?

Group Decision

Work in groups of five. • *The people in this picture are looking for a video to watch together tonight.* • *What kind of video does each person prefer?* • *What kind of video will they enjoy together?* • *Report your decision to the class.*

Partner Interview

Partner's name _____

Practice these questions with your teacher. • *Then ask your partner.*

1. Do you ever rent videos?
2. Where is the best place to rent videos in your neighborhood?
3. What kind of videos do you like?
4. What kind of tv programs do you like?
5. Do you ever watch late night tv?
6. Which do you like better: to watch tv or to watch videos? Why?

Community Activity

Use a real tv schedule from the newspaper. • *Choose one day of the week.* • *Decide which programs to watch for that day.* • *Write the name, channel, and time of each program.* • *Report your decision to the class.*

MOVIES

1. actor
2. actress
3. aisle
4. audience
5. refreshment stand
6. screen
7. ticket
8. usher
9. video game

_____
_____
_____

176

Class Discussion

1. What was the last movie you saw?
2. What movies are in the theaters now?
3. What new movie do you want to see?
4. What do you like to eat and drink at the movies?
5. Do you like to play video games in the movie lobby?

Group Role Play

Work in groups of four. • *Choose one of these situations.* • *Write a role play.* • *Include roles for everyone.* • *Present your conversation to the class.*

two friends going to a movie together
a woman selling tickets
an usher collecting tickets
a man selling refreshments

Conversation Squares

First write your own answers. • *Then ask your partners the questions.* • *Write their answers.* • *Compare your group answers with other groups.* • *How many students have the same favorites?*

Favorite	You:	Partner 1:	Partner 2:
Movie			
Actress			
Actor			
Comedian			

INDIVIDUAL SPORTS

1. aerobics
2. bicycling
3. bowling
4. boxing
5. golf
6. gymnastics
7. hiking
8. jogging
9. running
10. skating
11. skiing
12. swimming
13. tennis
14. working out
15. wrestling
16. yoga
_____
_____
_____

Group Survey

Ask everyone in your group these questions. • *Write all the answers.* • *Compare your group opinions with the rest of the class.*

1. Which is the most difficult? _____
2. Which is the easiest? _____
3. Which is the most exciting? _____
4. Which is the most dangerous? _____
5. Which is the most fun to watch on tv.? _____
6. Which of these sports is exercise? _____

Class Game: *"What is your favorite way to exercise?"*

Think. • *Write.* • *Fold your paper.* • *Make a pile of papers.* • *Open one.* • *Ask "What am I doing?"* • *Have the class guess the exercise.*

Community Activity

Where can you play a sport? • *Use the telephone directory.* • *Find out this information:*

Is there a	YES	NO	WHERE?
1. skating rink?	_____	_____	_____
2. bowling alley?	_____	_____	_____
3. swimming pool?	_____	_____	_____
4. tennis court?	_____	_____	_____
5. golf course?	_____	_____	_____
6. ski area?	_____	_____	_____
7. bicycle trail?	_____	_____	_____

TEAM SPORTS

1. baseball	9. basketball	17. football	24. soccer
2. base	10. basket	18. coach	25. goal
3. catch	11. dribble	19. down	26. kick
4. hit	12. foul	20. field goal	27. net
5. out	13. free throw	21. goal post	28. referee
6. pitch	14. hoop	22. tackle	
7. run	15. pass	23. touchdown	
8. umpire	16. shoot		

Group Discussion

Work in groups of eight. • *Discuss these questions.* • *Report your answers to the class.*

1. Did you ever play on a team? Which one(s)?
2. When did you play?
3. Where did you play?
4. What position did you play?
5. Do you like to watch team sports on tv? What do you like to watch?
6. Do you ever go to a sports event? Which ones do you like to attend?
7. Do you have a favorite team? Which one?

Conversation Squares

First write your answers. • *Then ask your partners the questions.* • *Write their answers.* •
Compare your group answers with other groups. • *How many students have the same favorites?*

Favorite	You:_____	Partner 1:_____	Partner 2:_____
Sport	_____	_____	_____
Team	_____	_____	_____
Player	_____	_____	_____

Community Activity

What sport season is it now? • *Which teams are winning?* • *Choose a game to watch on tv and report to the class.* • *Who played?* • *Who won?* • *What was the score?* • *What interesting things happened?*

Cross-Cultural Exchange

What is the most popular team sport in your country? • *Who is the most popular sports hero in your country?*

AT THE PARK

1. cane	6. path	11. squirrel
2. doll carriage	7. pigeon	12. stroller
3. frisbee	8. sandbox	13. swings
4. jungle gym	9. see saw	14. water fountain
5. kite	10. slide	

_____
_____
_____
_____
_____

Find Someone Who

Review the vocabulary with your teacher. • *Fill in the name of someone who. . .*

1. _____ likes to jog in the park.
2. _____ likes to feed the birds in the park.
3. _____ likes to feed the squirrels in the park.
4. _____ likes to take children to the playground.
5. _____ likes to fly a kite.

Strip Story

Work in groups of four. • Look at the pictures. • Decide what is happening. • Write captions for the story. • Tell the story to the class.

Cross-Cultural Exchange

What do parks look like in your hometown? • When do people go to the park? • What do they do in there? • What is the name of a famous park in your county? • Describe it to the class.

TAKING A TRIP

1. by airplane	6. on a cruise ship	11. tour	_____
2. by bus	7. passport	12. travel brochure	_____
3. by train	8. sightseeing	13. trip	_____
4. camera	9. suitcase		_____
5. luggage/baggage	10. ticket		_____

What's the Story?

Work in groups of three. • Write a story about this picture. • Everyone in the group should contribute at least one line. • Read your story to the class.

Group Vocabulary Challenge

Work in groups of three or four. • What would you pack for a trip to a tropical island? • Make a list. • Read your group's list to the class. • Make a list of all vocabulary on the board. • The group with the longest list is the winner!

Group Discussion

Work in groups of five. • *Discuss these questions.* • *Report the answers to the class.*

1. What do you like to do on vacation?
2. How do you prefer to travel?
3. Do you visit your family on vacation? Where do they live?
4. Do you ever travel to another country? Where do you go?
5. What is the most beautiful place you have ever been to?

Write

Imagine you are on vacation. • *Complete the postcard.* • *Address it to your English class.* • *Read it to your class.*

Hi.

　　　Having a wonderful time in _____. I'm enjoying the _____. The weather is _____.

_____.

Place stamp here

Cross-Cultural Exchange

What is the best place to visit in your country? • *Tell the class about it it.* • *Do you have a postcard or photo of a special place in your country?* • *Bring the card or photo to class.* • *Tell the class about the place.* • *Make a bulletin board with everyone's postcard.*

AT THE BEACH

1. beach	8. rescuing	15. sunburn
2. beach towel	9. sailboat	16. suntan
3. beach umbrella	10. sand	17. surf
4. drowning	11. sand castle	18. surfboard
5. lifeguard	12. shovel	19. water skiing
6. life preserver	13. speedboat	
7. pail	14. sunbathing	

What's the Story?

Decide who you would like to be in this picture. • *Write a story.* • *Read your story to the class.*

186

CAMPING

1. backpack	7. mosquito	13. sleeping bag
2. bear	8. porcupine	14. snake
3. campfire	9. quills	15. sunrise
4. deer	10. raccoon	16. tent
5. fox	11. set up camp	17. trailer
6. lantern	12. skunk	18. wild animal

Class Discussion

1. Do any wild animals live near you? Which ones?
2. What wild animals live in your country?
3. What would you do if you met any of these animals?

Partner Activity

Partner's name _____

Look at the picture. • Finish the story. • Write captions. • Compare your story with others in the class.

THE LIBRARY

1. author	7. encyclopedia	13. periodicals
2. card catalog	8. late fine	14. reference
3. check out	9. librarian	15. stacks(shelves)
4. circulation desk	10. library card	16. subject
5. dictionary	11. magazine	17. title
6. due	12. overdue	

Partner Vocabulary Challenge

Partner's name _____

Make a list of all the people in the library and what they are doing. • *Compare your list with another partner group.*

Community Activity

With your class, plan a visit to the library in your school or your community. • *Make a list of some questions to ask.*

SCHOOL

Class Discussion

1. What other courses can you take where you study English?
2. Have you ever taken another course? Which one? When is it offered?
3. Would you like to take another course? What course?
4. Do many adults go to school in your country? What kinds of courses can adults take?

Group Game: *Gossip!*

Work in groups of eight. • *Choose a leader.* • *Close your books.* • *What are the people saying?*

Leader: (To the first student) Read the secret on page 203. Close your book. Whisper the secret to the student sitting next to you.
Next Student: Whisper the secret to the student sitting next to you, etc.
Last Student: Write the secret on the board or tell the class.
Class: Check the secret on page 203. Which group had the most accurate secret?

Community Activity

Get a catalog from an adult school. • *Pick out courses you would like to take.* • *How much English is required?* • *What did most of the students in the class choose?* • *Sign up and enjoy!!*

REVIEW

Partner Interview

Partner's name _____

Ask your partner.

1. What is today's date?
2. What is your name?
3. What do you like to do in your leisure time?
4. Where do you prefer to spend your time?
5. How often do you watch TV?
6. What do you watch on TV?
7. What is your favorite physical exercise?
8. What would you like to try someday?
9. What do you never want to do?
10. Where would you like to visit someday?

Write

Write about your partner in your journal.

_____
(1)

My partner's name is _____. When he/she
(2)

has leisure time, he/she likes to _____. He/she
(3)

prefers to spend time _____. He/she watches
(4)

TV _____. When he/she watches TV, he/she prefers
(5)

to watch _____.
(6)

His/her favorite physical exercise is _____. He/She
(7)

would like to try _____ someday, but he/she never
(8)

wants to try_____. He/She would like to visit _____
(9)   (10)

someday.

Tell the Class

Read your journal to the class.   •   Tell the class about your partner.

Cross-Cultural Exchange

Bring in some typical music from your country.   •   Tell the class about the music.   •   Is there a special dance for the music?   •   Teach it to the class.

190

APPENDIX

AFRICA

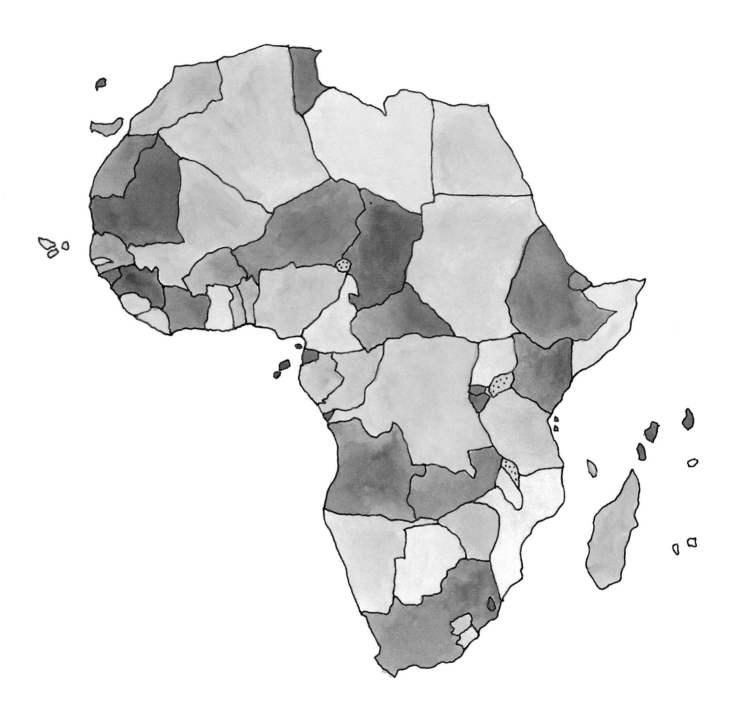

ASIA AND AUSTRALIA

EUROPE

NORTH AMERICA, CENTRAL AMERICA, SOUTH AMERICA

UNITED STATES OF AMERICA (U.S.A.) AND CANADA

COMMON NAMES/NICKNAMES

Notice that some men's and women's nicknames are the same or have the same pronunciation. Many nicknames for children end in -y. Some names do not have nicknames. Add more names to the list.

MEN

GIVEN NAME	NICKNAMES
Albert	Al, Bert
Alexander	Alex, Al
Alfred	Al, Fred
Andrew	Andy, Drew
Anthony	Tony
Arnold	Arnie
Brian	_____
Christopher	Chris
Daniel	Dan, Danny
David	Dave, Davey
Edward	Ed, Eddie, Ted, Teddy
Elvis	_____
Eugene	Gene
Francis	Frank, Frankie
Franklin	Frank, Frankie
Gerald	Gerry, Jerry
James	Jim, Jimmy
John	Jack, Johnny
Joseph	Joe, Joey
Lawrence	Larry
Lee	_____
Louis	Lou, Louie
Mark	_____
Martin	Marty
Matthew	Matt, Matty
Melvin	Mel
Michael	Mike, Mikey
Nathaniel	Nat
Nicholas	Nick, Nicky
Patrick	Pat
Paul	_____
Peter	Pete, Petey
Richard	Dick, Rick, Rich, Ricky
Robert	Bob, Bobby, Rob, Robbie
Sean/Shawn	_____
Stephen	Steve, Stevie
Terrence	Terry
Thomas	Tom, Tommy
Theodore	Ted, Teddy
William	Bill, Will, Billy, Willy

WOMEN

GIVEN NAME	NICKNAMES
Ann, Anne	Annie
Barbara	Barb, Barbie
Carol, Carole	_____
Carolyn	_____
Catherine	Cathy
Christine	Christie, Tina, Chrissy, Chris
Cynthia	Cindy
Dorothy	Dot, Dottie
Elaine	_____
Emily	_____
Elizabeth	Beth, Betsy, Betty, Liz
Faith	_____
Fay, Faye	_____
Frances	Fran
Gloria	_____
Helen	_____
Hope	_____
Jacqueline	Jackie
Jane	_____
Janet	Jan
Jean, Jeanne	Jeannie
Jeanette	_____
Jessica	Jess, Jessie
Joan	Joannie
Joanne	Jo
Judith	Judy
Kathleen	Kathy
Linda	_____
Lisa	_____
Margaret	Peggy, Peg, Maggie
Margery	Marj
Martha	Marty
Mary	_____
Maryanne	_____
Patricia	Pat, Patty, Patsy
Roberta	Bobbie
Rose	Rosie
Sally	_____
Sandra	Sandy
Sharon	Sherry
Susan	Sue, Susie
Teresa	Terry

NATIONS/NATIONALITIES

Notice that many nationalities end in *-ese, -ish, -an, -ian,* or *-i.* Add more nations and nationalities to the list.

NATION	NATIONALITY	NATION	NATIONALITY
	(-ese)		(-an)
Burma	Burmese	Chile	Chilean
China	Chinese	Cuba	Cuban
Japan	Japanese	The Dominican	Dominican
Lebanon	Lebanese	Republic	
Portugal	Portuguese	Germany	German
Senegal	Senegalese	Kenya	Kenyan
Sudan	Sudanese	Korea	Korean
Vietnam	Vietnamese	Mexico	Mexican
_____	_____	Puerto Rico*	Puerto Rican
_____	_____	South Africa	South African
		Uganda	Ugandan
	(-ian)	U.S.A. The United	American
Australia	Australian	States of America	
Brazil	Brazilian	Venezuela	Venezuelan
Canada	Canadian	_____	_____
Egypt	Egyptian	_____	_____
Ethiopia	Ethiopian		
Haiti	Haitian		(-i)
Hungary	Hungarian	Israel	Israeli
India	Indian	Kuwait	Kuwaiti
Indonesia	Indonesian	Pakistan	Pakistani
Iran	Iranian	Saudi Arabia	Saudi
Italy	Italian	Somalia	Somali
Nigeria	Nigerian	_____	_____
Panama	Panamanian	_____	_____
Peru	Peruvian		
Russia	Russian		irregular)
_____	_____	France	French
_____	_____	Germany	German
		Greece	Greek
	(-ish)	Netherlands	Dutch
Denmark	Danish	Switzerland	Swiss
England	English	Thailand	Thai
Ireland	Irish	_____	_____
Poland	Polish	_____	_____
Spain	Spanish		
Sweden	Swedish		
Turkey	Turkish		
_____	_____		
_____	_____		

PRINTING UPPER-CASE LETTERS (CAPITAL LETTERS)

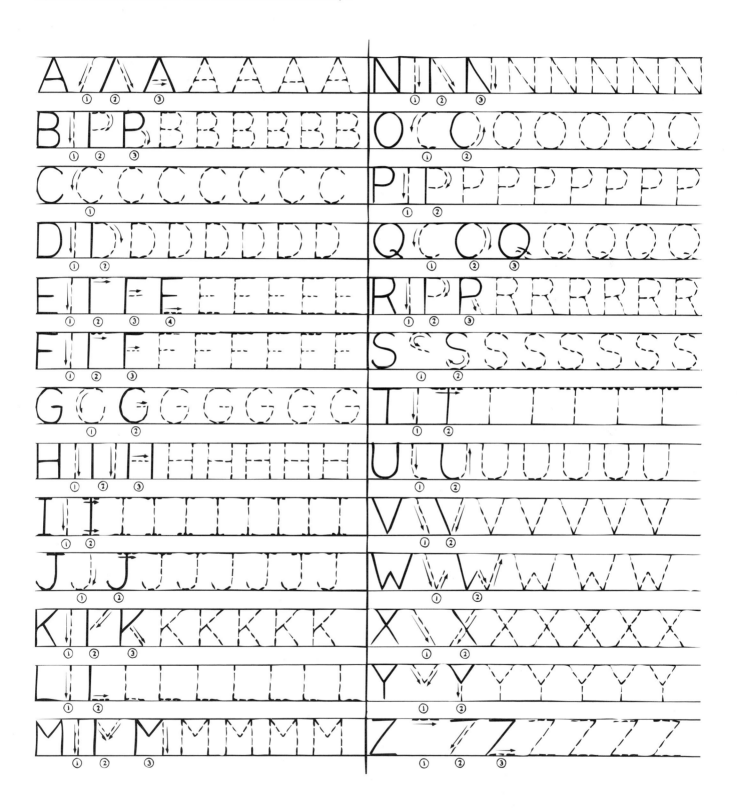

PRINTING LOWER-CASE LETTERS (SMALL LETTERS)

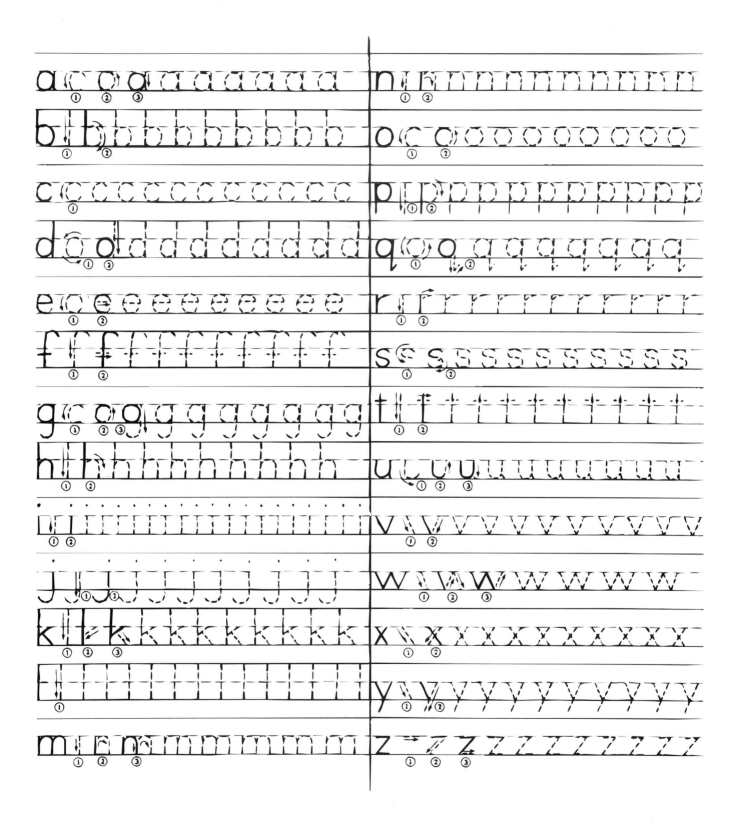

WRITING UPPER-CASE LETTERS
(CAPITAL LETTERS)

WRITING LOWER-CASE LETTERS (SMALL LETTERS)

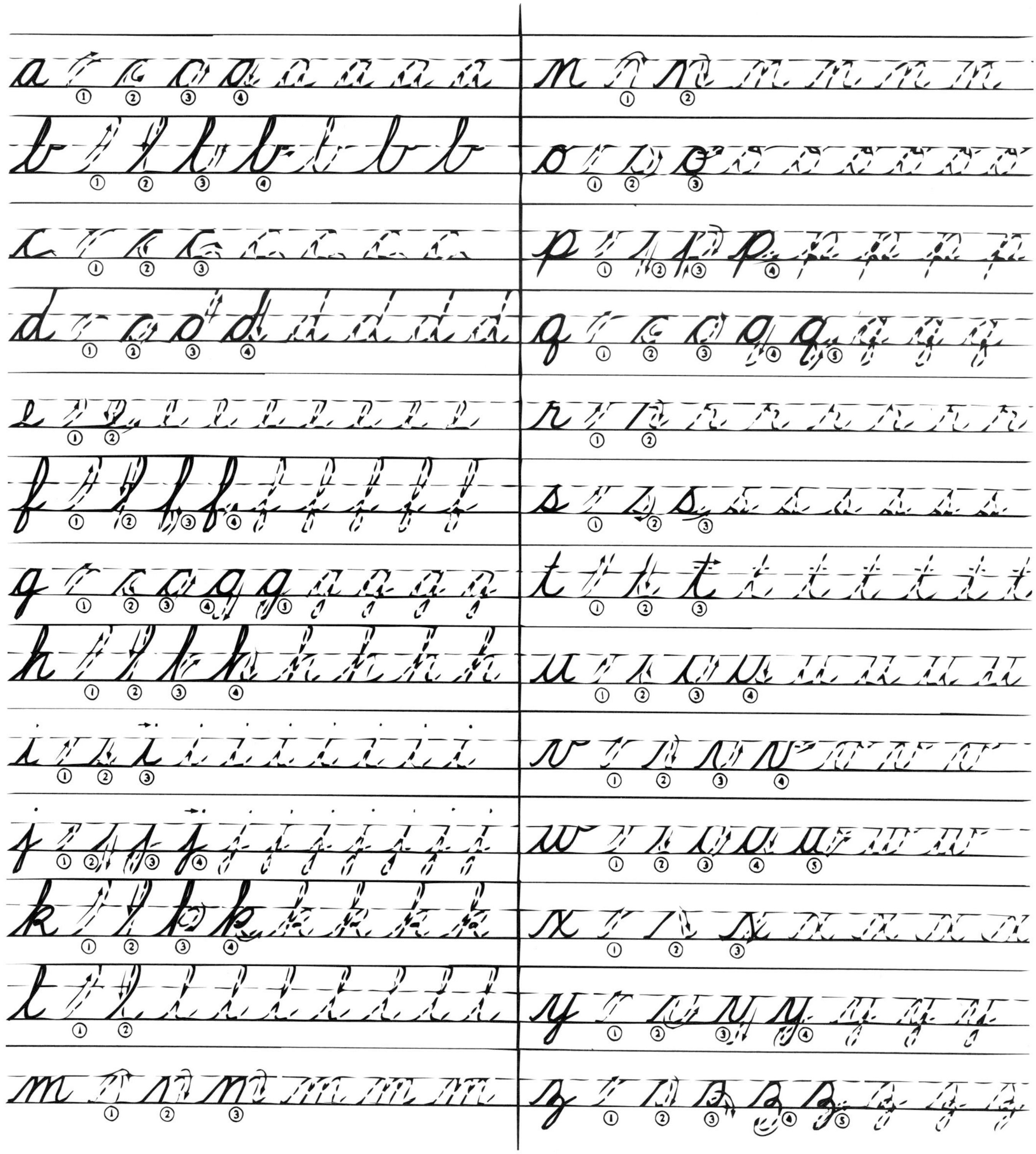

GOSSIP SECRETS

CHAPTER 5, PAGE 63: *City or Country*

I was born and grew up on a farm in the country. It was very peaceful and beautiful. Then I went to the city with my husband. I did not like the city. It was too noisy and crowded. Now my family and I live in a town in the mountains. We are happy there.

CHAPTER 5, PAGE 71: *Living Room*

I love my living room. I stay in the living room all day. Sometimes I lie on the sofa and watch TV. Sometimes I listen to music and sleep in the armchair. Sometimes I walk on the coffee table and eat the plant there. I like to play with the pillow on the sofa and the lampshade on the lamp. I am a beautiful yellow cat.

CHAPTER 9, PAGE 163: *Medical Problem*

Last week a nineteen-year-old girl came to the hospital with her aunt. The girl was very weak and very tired. Her blood tests showed a problem, but she did not want treatment. Her religion was against medical treatment. The girl's aunt was angry. She said, "You must have treatment!" The girl said, "No. God will give me treatment." Then she and her aunt went away. They did not come back, so we don't know what happened.

CHAPTER 10, PAGE 189: *Going to School*

In January I started a computer course at a community college. The first class was very difficult. After class my car didn't start. It was snowing and cold. I was very unhappy. Fortunately, a student from my class helped me with my car. He helped me with the computer course, too. We studied together all semester. I got an "A" in the course, and next week we are getting married! What a wonderful semester!

SPEECH EVALUATION FORM

Speaker's Name: _____

Date: _____

Speech Topic: _____

	Needs Work	Satisfactory
Organization	_____	_____
Pronunciation	_____	_____
Vocabulary	_____	_____
Eye Contact	_____	_____
Visual Aids	_____	_____
Best Part of Speech	_____	

Evaluator's Name: _____

AUDIENCE EVALUATION FORM

Speaker's Name: _____

Date: _____

Speech Topic: _____

	Needs Work	Satisfactory
Attentiveness	_____	_____
Quietness	_____	_____
Eye Contact	_____	_____
Appropriateness of Questions	_____	_____
Form of Questions	_____	_____
Number of Questions	_____	_____
Responsiveness	_____	_____

Evaluator's Name: _____

NOTE: You may make as many copies of these forms as you need.

ALPHABETICAL INDEX TO PICTURE DICTIONARY VOCABULARY